mr. towers
of
london
a life in show business

HARRY ALAN TOWERS

BearManor Media
Albany, Georgia

Published in the USA by:
BearManor Media
PO Box 1129
Duncan, OK 73534-1129
www.BearManorMedia.com

ISBN 1-59393-235-9

Printed in the United States of America

Design and Layout by Allan T. Duffin.

Table of Contents

Dedication vii

Prologue ix

Introduction xiii

1. Early Days 1

2. My Journey Continues 13

3. A Diversion: The Night Life in London 25

4. New York, New York — and Elsewhere 31

5. King of Radio, But for How Long? 39

6. Success, and then Disaster 43

7. I Am a Film Producer 53

8. Let's Make More Movies 87

9. Some Call It Euro-Pudding 95

10. Going Back 103

11. Action and More Action 109

12. Films Come in Cannes 113

13. My Eyes are Red 119

14. Movies I Haven't Made — Yet 127

15. All the Spoons in All the Glasses 131

Epilogue: Au Revoir — Not Goodbye 135

Post Script 137

To Maria 139

Index 141

Dedication

This biography is dedicated with gratitude to:

Margaret Miller, my strong mother; Harry P. Towers, my wonderful father, and Maria, my beloved wife, who has always been there for me since we first met, which is nearly half a century ago. I love her with all my heart.

I want to take this opportunity to thank all the wonderful people who celebrated my 84th birthday with me at 84. Hallam St. in London. as well as everybody who has contributed and enhanced this last decade for me including Kris, Karen, Kathy and Sylvia and everybody who was with us on my 88th birthday which I spent in comfort with my beloved Maria in the "Pursuit of Happiness".

Special thanks to Hunter Phoenix, who has enriched my recent years with her beauty, intelligence and sensitivity apart from being a very good actress and writer as well as great friend to Maria.

Prologue

I also want to thank all the men and women who have lived and died, loved and suffered before me and, who made it possible for me to be an observer and small contributor to the "The Rise and Fall of the British Empire" with all its power and glory that I, in part, was allowed to witness.

The Power reached its climax in 1898 with the Diamond Jubilee of Queen Victoria. It was a spectacular occasion. Joseph Chamberlain was high in the government of those days. He had, for the first time, arranged an assembly of troops from all over the British Empire.

They came from Canada, Australia and New Zealand, South Africa and of course, the Indian Empire. It was an impressive occasion as they marched through the streets of London, followed by the horse drawn carriage that brought Queen Victoria to the steps of St. Paul's Cathedral.

The queen was too frail to enter the Cathedral, so the service was conducted on the steps of St. Paul's. Afterward, the queen returned, in State, to Buckingham Palace. There Victoria wrote in her memoirs

"This was the most exciting day of my life".

It was just as well that all the celebrations were so successful, as within three years Queen Victoria was dead.

Her funeral in 1901 was one of the last great State occasions for the British Empire, though many of a similar nature would follow. Queen Victoria's son, King Edward III, succeeded her.

King Edward III was very fond of sport and the ladies, a man who liked a good time. In one week, the king achieved more than most diplomats can in a life time. The king went to France to cement the "Entente Cordial" that offered a challenge to the now growing German Empire.

The king died before World War One began, but his legacy, the Edwardian Era, has survived for long thereafter.

At the time of the commencement of World War One, George V was on the throne, with his fine wife, Queen Mary. Their son, the Prince of Wales, participated in a very well protected fashion in World War One.

When it ended, the Prince of Wales went on a worldwide tour, with his good friend, Lord Louis Mountbatten.

Meantime in Paris, the Treaty of Versailles was haggled over and finally signed thus sowing the seeds for World War Two.

The period between the two wars, was a time of stagnation, including the Deep Depression. When World War Two finally broke out, it was a tired and unpopular Prime Minister, Neville Chamberlain, who spoke the words over the BBC, "We are now at war with Germany."

This was again, "the war to end all wars." There were no delusions this time, it was a bloody contest. From the bombing of Pearl Harbor, it became a war in which, truly, the whole world was involved.

Back in 1937, the Abdication Crises brought to the throne a brave, but stuttering George VI. Incidentally, few remember, that NATO, the North Atlantic Treaty Organization, was born on a Battle Ship off the coast of Newfoundland. When President Roosevelt and Winston Churchill met, to declare the values in which they both believed.

When World War Two concluded, it was not the end of war.

No one was deluding themselves this time, as Winston Churchill, declared in a famous speech, "An iron curtain now extends from Stetin to the Baltic."

Thus the Cold War began and lasted until the fall of the Berlin Wall.

George VI died early and was succeeded by our present Queen Elisabeth II who may, like her mother, live to be one hundred. Thus the reign of the queen's son, Prince Charles, the Prince of Wales, may in turn, be brief.

Prince Charles' and Princess Diana's older son, Price William shows promise. After all the Brigade of Guards, one of the few remaining emblems of royalty has managed to keep in step with the times.

The moment had arrived, when America became the world's only superpower.

One could now say that the Pax Britannica has ended and the Pax Americana, which has loomed so long on the horizon, was now a complete reality.

The British Empire, by the time of Prime Minister Margaret Thatcher, was reduced to a few minor dependencies, such as Gibraltar and the Falkland Island.

Nonetheless, Britain went to war over the Falkland Islands and it was a very proud Margaret Thatcher, who exalted in the defeat of the enemy.

Thus we move to the end of our story.

After 9/11, Prime Minister Tony Blair, tried to maintain the special relationship between Britain and the United States by agreeing to the war in Iraq.

It was an equal disaster for, both, Tony Blair and President George W. Bush. The closing stages of our history are a work still in progress, but if we are to mark the moment, when the page of history turns, we should make it the occasion, when the British troops are withdrawn from Iraq, probably under the Premiership of Gordon Brown.

Thus we have followed the trail for many years, which saw the rise and fall of the British Empire.

I miss it greatly.

Prologue

We can only celebrate it with "Pomp and Circumstance," in the belief, that these great times have a place in our history that cannot easily be forgotten.

God has seen the end of the British Empire and, hopefully an equally successful Pax Americana will take its place. Only time can tell, but that's always the case.

Time can tell and in time it will.

Introduction

A t the age of twenty five I wrote a book about me called *Show Business*.

At the age of forty, through tragic necessity, I also wrote about myself.

I have, for many years, resisted the suggestions that I should embark on a third and, no doubt, final attempt, to write an autobiography.

The fact that I am now doing so could be a bad sign.

Up to now, I have been so heavily concentrating on living my life that, if today, I am prepared to even consider writing about it, could it mean that I have lost interest in living it?

There is, however, a more inspiring reason.

I am finally listening to my wife and accepting her advice.

Above all, I think, it is time I revealed more of the truth about the most dramatic periods of my life.

Sex has played quite a considerable part in my adult life, though I have never benefited financially from the sexual activities of the ladies I have met and known.

I am going to tell anything I can remember and, wherever possible, I will use the actual names, except when it is necessary for the protection of privacy of an individual or organization.

Maria, my wife, believes that the origin for my sexual behavior may have something to do with my mother, who naturally had a rather Victorian attitude towards sex and the "forbidden" has greater allure.

Also, growing up backstage as a child, brought me face to face with many young and beautiful women in their various costumes and glittering show outfits. I was enthralled and totally fascinated.

Considering the enormous part glamorous women have played in my life some positive, some challenging, I can offer the alternative title: *Mr. Towers of Everywhere—Around the Girls in Eighty Years.*

"H.A.T.–This is Your Life"—devised and written by Harry Alan Towers.

Chapter One
Early Days

My first memories are pleasant but vague. My parents loved each other. My feelings toward my mother were somewhat mixed. On a table in her bedroom stood a beautiful portrait photograph of her, inscribed in my father's handwriting, "Little white bird."

I was said to have responded with, "Big, black eagle"

My father had started life as an engineering apprentice. He had gone to Canada to work for the Westinghouse Company. They were building the first hydro-electric power plant at Niagara Falls. There, according to his own account, he ran away from his job to join a traveling troupe of players. He ended up back in London on the business side of what he loved most in life—the theatre.

He moved from one job to another, first in the box office, then in a managerial capacity. His employers were famous – Sir Herbert Beerbohm Tree, Mrs. Rupert D'Oyly Carte and the Vedrenne Barker management of the Royal Court Theatre, where the plays of George Bernard Shaw were first performed. My father, who knew Shaw, had persuaded him to grant him the touring rights on *You Never Can Tell* that featured a young Lynn Fontaine.

My father's life was rich and varied, including one summer, my family's first connection with motion pictures, which was when my dad toured the villages of North Wales with the first cinema projector they had ever seen and a print of "Queen Victoria's Funeral." When World War One broke out, my father joined the Royal Pay Corps and ended up in the Lancashire town of Preston, where he met my mother.

My mother came from a good family of Scottish origin. Her father, a baker, was mayor of the seaport where my mother was born, Fleetwood, Lancashire. She soon left Preston and became an officer in the WAAC, the Women's Army Auxiliary Corps, and was posted to France. Mother enjoyed a good life, but had not forgotten about my father.

When mother came back home they got married soon after the war ended. My parents set up home in a large, thirteen room house in Balham, a South London suburb, where I was to be born. My mother knew nothing of the theatre, but took a "walk on" part in the touring version of *The Merry Widow* that my father was managing.

My childhood was enlivened by traveling with my mother and father on theatrical tours. Thus, early in life, I gained an extensive knowledge of England, Wales, Scotland and Ireland, but confined entirely to "Number One Theatrical Touring Dates." I knew, and know, nothing of the beauty of Devon and Cornwall and in Scotland; I have only once been North of Edinburgh and Glasgow.

When not on tour with my mother and father, I attended Balham Grammar School. One of the two headmasters and part owner of this private school, Charles Packwood, was to have a profound influence on my life. Together with the master of the form where I first studied, a Mr. Bennett, they enhanced my knowledge of English history and the theatre, gained from my father.

I still possess today the red leather bound collection of the plays of William Shakespeare, originally given to me as a school prize.

Every year at Hamilton Hall on Balham High Street, on the opposite side to the school, Charles Packwood staged an entertainment for the parents and friends of his boys. I recall the first year when he staged one of the comedy interludes from Shakespeare's *A Midsummer Night's* Dream, in which I played Wall in *Pyramus and Thisbe*.

Next year, it was the turn of Cervantes and I played Sancho Panza in *Don Quixhote*.

The following year it was much more ambitious, a revue which I co-wrote with Mr. Packwood, and in which I appeared disguised as an old actor who related the story of a friend who aspired to be an actor "who went on as Hamlet and came off as Omelette, my very first successful gag.

Thank you Mr. Packwood, for the start you helped to give me in entering "show business," the only business I know.

We moved from Balham, first to Morden and then to South Side Clapham Common, as my father's fortunes steadily declined. My very first job was with a certain R. G. Jones, who operated a single van, mounted with four Tannoy loudspeakers. Mr. Jones and his wife lived in a caravan in a field near Morden. The van was for hire. I went with the van.

When Oswald Mosley's black shirts threatened the Jewish community in the East End of London, we supported the Jewish Brown Shirts. When times were bad Mr Jones purchased from a wholesale chemist a large jar of cough syrup. Mrs Jones and my mother would then fill tiny bottles with the cough cure, which were then individually labelled "Magnet Lightning Cough Cure."

We, Mr Jones the van and I, would then, together, tour London's "twenty thousand streets beneath the sky" and sell our wares. Whilst Mr Jones solicited customers, house by house, I sat inside the van and gave the "spiel" into the loudspeakers.

One day the police intervened and were surprised to find inside the van, giving the "spiel," a twelve year old boy.

Mr Jones and I were arrested

In a panic, my mother arrived, and pleaded with the police to drop any charge against me, so that I would have no criminal record. She succeeded.

In school, I had developed an interest in acting in the school plays and revues and had studied at the well known establishment of Italia Conti, where Noel Coward and Gertrude Lawrence were among the more famous ex pupils.

I developed my own vaudeville act.

I appeared in a Children's Variety Show at the Ambassador Theatre, under the management of Basil Dean and, in the dressing room which I shared with a young actor. I watched him applying lipstick. I decided, there and then, that the life of an actor was not for me.

But I had to earn a living and endured, briefly, a series of jobs with Thomas Cook, the travel agents, Keith Prowse, the theatre ticket vendors, before, finally, finding what I was looking for. In between the two World Wars, British broadcasting and the pioneer television service was the monopoly of the BBC. The only competition came from the so called pirate radio stations in Luxembourg and Normandy, whose income was from advertisers. I applied for a job with the International Broadcasting Company, who managed Radio Normandy and I went for an interview at their London offices in Hallam Street, just behind Broadcasting House. The interview—and the street—were to play a major role in my life.

The job I was given was in Continuity Acceptance where I had to review and check the entire program content. I soon developed it into my own little world. Most of the program content of Radio Normandy and its richer and larger competitor, Radio Luxembourg was prerecorded in London. My job was to assemble and check the program material. For somebody as curious and ambitious as myself, it was a perfect role and I was extremely successful.

I was soon offered a better job with the radio station in France, but my parents didn't want me to go abroad. I was almost nineteen when World War II broke out in September of 1939. I felt my world had come to an end when Radio Normandy went out of business. My mother had gone back to the Women's Army and my father to the Royal Army Pay Corp. I was all alone in London.

I wrote a script called *Hot Cinders*. I sent it to the BBC and they bought it.

Shortly afterwards, when it was broadcast, it was heard by an ex colleague from IBC (the International Broadcasting Company), a producer, Tom Ronald, then working for the BBC in Bristol. He suggested I should write something for the Variety Department. Soon, I was as busy as a beaver.

Writing, mainly comedy, but writing, writing and more writing…

I had volunteered for the Royal Air Force and my first destination was Number Ten Recruit Centre, the largest in England, in Blackpool, a resort town I knew well. By the time I arrived in Blackpool, I already had a private office, doubling as a bedroom, and a personal secretary, who happened to be the daughter of one of my "soon to be" commanding officers.

I had failed my air crew tests and joined the staff of Number Ten R.C. and busied myself in my private office, churning out scripts for the BBC. It was 1941. I had, by now become a principal supplier of comedy scripts to the Variety Department, where my now good friend, Tom Ronald, put me to work providing the material for new series for prime time broadcast.

When I had started as a comedy writer, the BBC frequently engaged famous music hall stars to appear as guests. Not aware that they were expected to provide their own material, I used to create brand new sketches and comedy characters, based on my knowledge of their own existing, and somewhat threadbare, music hall acts.

I became a hero to the stars, who, in many cases, had been living off the same jokes for many years during which they had toured the vaudeville theatres. Remember, at this period, there were still nearly fifty active "Music Halls"; one in every town.

The outbreak of the war had left a number of American variety acts stranded in England; others elected to stay where they had homes and a professional career. These included such

American names as Bebe Daniels and Ben Lyon and a comedy trio, Forsythe, Seaman and Farrell, billed as a "Ton of Fun," who became my special friends.

I wrote a successful series in which they starred and, when in London, I was their guest at, what seemed to me, luxury apartments in Maida Vale. Every weekend I disappeared, in civilian clothes, from my base in Blackpool, to visit the BBC Variety Department, moved, for security reasons, to North Wales. The head of the BBC Variety Department in those wartime days was John Watt. I cannot remember whether it was I, or some other comedy writer who described him as "very bright for one Watt."

My next task was to turn out more difficult than I thought. I was to write six, weekly, one hour comedy shows for a very popular variety act with Arthur Lucan and Kitty McShane: "Old Mother Reilly Take the Aire." When we first met, Arthur endeavored to inspire me, by telling me, "Harry, we had a very big success last year by doing our act in 'Northern Music Hall' from the Argyll, Birkenhead—thirty minutes of uninterrupted laughter, without a word of dialogue."

I too, was speechless. Their standard Variety Act, which they had been doing for many years, took place late at night, in the kitchen of their home. In the distance, we heard a church bell strike three. Mother Reilly (Arthur Lucan) exclaimed, "One o'clock three times. I'll separate her from her breath."

When Kitty McShane, Arthur's wife, arrives, Arthur starts to belt her with crockery, of which there was plenty on the shelves, until he is down to his last possession—his china teapot. As Arthur turns to show us the pot, he accidentally smashes it against the wall and is left holding only the handle. The act required two cases of reject china dishware, which was demolished in the twice nightly performances.

In their private lives, Arthur and Kitty had constant arguments. Late one night in Morecombe, where they were appearing, Kitty threw a solid glass ash tray at Arthur, which only narrowly missed me. I got out fast, while I still could. Sometime, after the radio series concluded successfully, they split up.

However, it was much more heartbreaking for Arthur, who had assigned the entire rights for the act to Kitty, when he had the doleful experience of having to take a seat in the pit of the Middlesex Music Hall in London, where "Old Mother Reilly" was billed and seeing, an Irish tenor, who was currently sleeping with Kitty, performing his own act and wearing his own wardrobe. That must have felt really terrible.

My mother, who had become a senior officer in the Women's Army, the ATS, was stationed in Lancashire and I would sometimes collect her in my rented limo and take her with me to North Wales. On one occasion, as we passed through Liverpool, the air raid sirens sounded. My mother wanted to get out of the car and into an air raid shelter, but I grabbed her and pulled her back into the car, as we zoomed through the tunnel beneath the Mersey River.

Our home on the south side of Clapham Common had been destroyed during the blitz and mother decided we needed a new home. Blackpool was a holiday resort with many hotels and traditional boarding houses and there were no apartment blocks. We rented the top floor of a spacious house in the fashionable South Shore district.

My mother, who apparently could always do whatever she liked in the ATS, promptly became the ATS recruiting officer for Lancashire, based in Blackpool and we moved into our new premises.

I was still only an aircraftsman, the lowest rank in the RAF, and was glad to be living in comfort in the safe haven of Blackpool during the blitz. In addition to my regular contributions to the Variety Department, I found homes for my scripts all over the BBC.

I had a finger in every pie, including the BBC's most popular wartime comedy series *ITMA – It's That Man Again*. When the series went into its second season, I suggested to the resident writer, Ted Kavanagh, the idea of placing its action in a mythical seaside resort, called "Foaming at the Mouth." Henceforth, whenever its star, Tommy Handley, was addressed as "Mr. Mayor," the BBC paid me the handsome sum of five guineas.

The insistence on using my full triple barreled name and the distinctive credit of "devised and written by" had, by now, made me a household name, to the extent that, on one occasion, in a satirical revue on the BBC, reference was made to the Nine O'clock News, as being "devised and written by Harry Alan Towers."

In Blackpool, the RAF mounted a weekly stage show at the Winter Garden Theatre, "Contact" that featured the many theatrical performers serving with the RAF in Blackpool, including a young Music Hall star, Max Wall, basically a comedy dancer, whose Music Hall billing had been "The Boy with Obedient Feet."

My one time boss at the IBC, Frank Lamping, had become an RAF officer.

Among his duties was liaison with ENSA, the wartime organization that provided concert party entertainment for the forces at home and overseas. Among ENSA'S activities was a fledgling project to record such entertainment shows and distribute the programs to radio stations overseas, which had been established to entertain the forces.

Frank was an administrator without any creative experience. He asked me if I would organize a talent group which could come to London and record some programs. I jumped at the opportunity, organized the project and brought Max Wall, plus a supporting cast and a full orchestra conducted by a talented organist, Sidney Torch, to London's Fortune Theatre, where we recorded three half hour shows in one afternoon before a live audience.

Frank was impressed and delighted and asked me if I would like to be posted to London, to help him in his job. It was 1942.

Moving to London, I had been instructed by my mother's to find a suitable apartment on the ground floor of a concrete building, with an air raid shelter. Instead, I leased a beautiful apartment in an old brick building, on the fourth floor of 84 Hallam Street. There was no air raid shelter.

Meantime, we had to dispose of the balance of the lease of our apartment in Blackpool. I advertised the availability of this unique and desirable property in the local newspaper and the phone never stopped ringing. Finally, an applicant arrived at the door step in an RAF limo with a motor cycle escort. It was Air Commodore Howard Williams, the officer in command at Blackpool, at that time the largest RAF establishment in the world. He promptly became the tenant of Aircraftsman Towers.

In London, my mother and I took up our occupancy of flat 9, 84 Hallam Street, which was already a famous address. Ed Murrow, the pioneering American broadcaster, occupied a flat on the ground floor, and many of his legendary wartime broadcasts were made from the roof, where he had an excellent view of the blitz. Whenever we met we would talk about war time London. Except for one small move just around the corner to the Penthouse at 59 Devonshire Street, I have lived in the same area ever since.

I took every advantage of my return to London. I developed a highly successful, regular feature for the BBC: *March of the Movies* where we interview everybody who was anybody in the film industry. Thus I was introduced to the world of cinema. Later, I wrote a book which was published under the same title.

My name had, by now, become so familiar on the air that rumors abounded, that I might be bribing officials at the BBC. To stop these rumors, I adopted, for part of my output, the nom de plume of Peter Welbeck, after the London telephone exchange. I am still using this name today for my work as a script writer.

The year I arrived in London, a brilliant writer, who had been the peace time head of the BBC Variety department, entered my life. It was Eric Maschwitz, whose fame as a lyric writer remains secure as the author of "These Foolish Things," "A Nightingale Sang in Berkeley Square" and "Room 504."

Eric was a senior officer in the British Army and also, as I learned by accident many years later, a trusted secret agent of MI5. He had undertaken a tour of the areas where British Forces where then serving in Africa, Europe (Italy), the Middle East, Asia and the Far East. He had discovered that the forces were operating a multitude of small radio stations, to entertain the troops and were in need of a constant supply of program material.

Over the weekend, I went to work and based on my experience with the IBC, developed an organizational structure for a combined operation by the RAF, the Navy and the Army working with ENSA, which I christened the Overseas Recorded Broadcasting Service, ORBS.

The following Monday, I sold the plan to an inter-service committee and became the Controller of Programs for the newly created ORBS. I was still only an Aircraftsman but was due for a promotion.

Russia had entered the war and I found myself organizing a gala broadcast concert from Her Majesty's Theater, in honor of Mrs. Winston Churchill's "Aid to Russia Fund," with Mrs. Churchill herself in the Royal Box. Also present was the Russian Ambassador, Mr. Ivan Maisky, and backstage, after the show, he commented on my modest rank. I was promoted on the spot to the rank of Corporal.

Whilst continuing my successful and quite lucrative career as a writer, ORBS offered me a wonderful opportunity. It was within my power to have talent in the forces drafted, on temporary assignment, to London. Before my promotion, I used to sign the Internal Memos with my own name, accompanied by "AC" for Aircraftsman.

The recipients, the commanding officers, believed it to be an abbreviation for Air Commodore.

But ORBS also gave me the opportunity to approach the biggest names in the theatre and the cinema and ask them to devote their services, which they did. A little surprised at my youth, they were impressed by my energy and knowledge. I realized quickly that I was building relationships for the future.

For the ORBS, I developed a series, *Personal Call* in which celebrities introduced other stars who had affected their lives. Noël Coward, who had agreed to become one of the celebrities, had suggested I contact Alfred Lunt and Lynne Fontaine, who were visiting London to star in a play Noël had written. They consented to appear and I asked Alfred Lunt if they had any suitable material.

"Material" he complained, "we are actors, not vaudeville performers; we don't have "material."

I remembered that the famous playwright, Terence Rattigan, was serving, I believed, rather unhappily, at a remote station of Coastal Command. He was very willing to be posted to London for a week, during which, at the Savoy Hotel, he wrote a short sketch for the Lunts that he ultimately developed into a play *Oh Mistress Mine*, in which they also starred and which had a very successful run in London and on Broadway.

I was already working creatively with the biggest and most popular entertainers in wartime Britain, including Old Mother Riley (the variety act of Lucan and McShane) George Formby and Gracie Fields. However, it was impossible to ignore the fact that I was living and working in wartime London, with the air raid sirens screaming their warning nearly every night and the fire of the burning buildings lighting up the sky.

Then, in the morning the King and Queen, who had continued to live in London throughout the war, would visit the ruins and talk to the desperate, homeless survivors. They were often accompanied by Winston Churchill. Despite the multitude of seemingly insurmountable problems, due to the efficiency of the Ministry of Food, nobody ever went hungry.

My recollections of wartime London are illuminated by memories of the shows I saw and the stars I met and who, in some cases, became my friends. One of them was Tommy Trinder, a wonderful character.

During the war, in *Happy and Glorious* at the London Palladium, Tommy had discovered that advertising was tax deductible. So he had large posters put up all over London with the slogan:

"If it's laughter you're after Trinder is the name, you lucky people".

He also had the same poster up in the East End of London in Yiddish.

Sid Field, making his London debut, in *Strike A New Note* at the Prince of Wales and, singing together with Zoe Gail: "I'm Going to Get Lit Up when the Lights go up in London," who was later to lead the crowd in a reprise from up above the Criterion Theatre on VE Night.

Sid's years in the provinces had given him a cynical attitude toward authority and, when making his first movie, he was told that waiting to talk to him on the phone was J. Arthur Rank about a long term contract. Sid's response was: "Give him an evasive answer. Tell him to fuck himself." His attitude, luckily, had no repercussions.

Hermione Gingold, in *Sweet and Low* at the Ambassadors Theatre, singing "Thanks, Yanks" was later to make a memorable appearance in a movie for me, *Rocket to the Moon*.

At the London Hippodrome, the musical *Lisbon Story* by Harry Parr Davies the accompanist of Gracie Fields was a great success.

The show was presented by George Black, whose literacy was not among his virtues. Featured in the advertising on the posters outside the theatre were quotes from a newspaper review "the most pretentious new musical in London." George Black had confused the word pretentious with the word prestigious.

Another great British actor I met during the war was Leslie Howard.

I went to interview him at Denham Film Studios, where he was producing and directing a film originally entitled *The Gentle Sex*. Leslie believed in making films at his own pace and he had stopped shooting for a week to complete some rewrites. Enquiring on the sound stage for directions to his office I met two relaxed stage hands who referred to their employer as "Mister Leisurely Howard." Very sadly Leslie was killed during the war when a German pilot shot down the civilian plane in which Leslie was returning to London from a lecture tour in Portugal.

It was rumored that a German spy in Lisbon thought that the special treatment Leslie Howard was receiving was directed at Winston Churchill returning from Casablanca where he had met with President Roosevelt. So Leslie Howard died for his country even if not in combat.

Meantime through *March of the Movies* and its host Leslie Mitchell, a very early television announcer and personality, I had developed a working association with the London Daily Mail and its executives.

I invented the concept of staging "events," usually on Sunday nights, which the BBC would be happy to broadcast, together with frequent mention of its sponsor, the "Daily Mail."

This led to a whole series of promotions which continued during and after the war, with the Daily Mail and other newspaper organizations, including the "News of the World" and the "Daily Telegraph."

I had reinvented commercial broadcasting.

Opposite our apartment in Hallam Street was a building occupied by the Air Ministry Unit, to which I was attached, though I seldom collected my pay. Every morning, in a silk dressing gown, I would dictate my correspondence and, most mornings, my superior officer in the building across the road would view me with curiosity. Finally, when I did collect my pay, he recognized me and inquired, with some suspicion:

"I know you. What's your job in the RAF?"

I murmured, "Security" and from then on the officer in question, when he sighted me again, would hurriedly concentrate on his work. I kept up my active career as a writer, continuing to contribute to the BBC whenever and wherever I saw an opportunity. My specialty was developing radio series which featured music hall stars.

Stanelli, perhaps little remembered today, was such a star. He was a front cloth comedian who, for the finale of his act, produced and played on his "hornchestra," a xylophone look alike adorned with motor horns tuned to the required pitch.

For Stanelli and his "hornchestra," I created a series called the *Calamity Club*. He had a co-star on the show, another well known variety act, Ted Andrews, whose billing was "Canada's Singing Troubadour" with Barbara, his wife, at the piano. Their infant daughter, who traveled with them, was Julie Andrews. Thus I first met the lady I should meet again as a star on Broadway.

The *Calamity Club* originated in the BBC studios in Manchester, but each week when we headed north, the Luftwaffe had the same idea. Thus, each week the *Calamity Club* found Manchester blacked out. It was indeed—a calamity.

There came the day when ORBS had attracted sufficient attention to be granted an establishment and I found myself promoted to officer's rank in the RAF; initially Pilot Officer and ultimately, Flying Officer.

Mother had become the ATS Recruiting Officer for London and to my delight our apartment became graced with a series of attractive secretaries. Around this time I devised and wrote for the BBC a program based on the many Australians who had a big success in Britain. These included Cyril Ritchard and Madge Elliot, stars of musical comedy, revue and broadcasting and Hardy Amies, the Queen's dressmaker. I called the tribute, to the girls and boys from "down under," *Over and Up*.

This brings me back to my mother.

In addition to her many other duties, mother kept the books for Towers of London. However, I noticed, but did not mention it to her, that on one occasion mother had included an item in the production accounts that was a little suspect. The bill was payable to "Hardy Amies and his Orchestra."

I was starting to contribute to the wartime history of broadcasting in Britain. Before the war, Richard Murdoch had starred together with Arthur Askey, in a popular BBC series *Band Wagon*. Unhappily serving as an administrative officer in the RAF, I brought him to London and introduced him to an amateur entertainer and successful business man, Wing Commander Kenneth Horne. I made it a trio with a sad faced singer, Sam Costa, immortalized by the catch phrase "Was there something?" and I launched *Much Binding in the March* still fondly remembered by its surviving audience.

Another war time legend to which I contributed was Dame Vera Lynn, the "Sweetheart of the Forces." The producer, an old friend from my IBC days, Howard Thomas, sent her to me to write the scripts.

I was late in arriving back at Hallam Street and found my mother interviewing the shy Cockney girl for the vacant job of our household help.

When I arrived, I quickly straightened out the misunderstanding.

It was around this time that mother had reason to complain, that my obsession with my business affairs had made me oblivious to the dangers of wartime London. On one occasion we had been together to a play in the West End. The play had been interrupted by the theatre manager's announcement, telling the audience that an air raid warning was in effect.

We stayed in our seats and, happily, there was no further news of the world outside. But, when we both left the theatre to go home, the anti-aircraft barrage was at its height and pieces of shrapnel were falling all around us.

I urged mother to ignore the danger and to take the tube as the safest and fastest way home. Mother did not approve, but came with me anyway. We got out at Regent's Park Station, only a few minutes walk from our apartment on Hallam Street. It had started to rain and as I didn't want my brand new Pilot Officer's uniform to get wet, I hurried mother along—again she was not pleased.

The war was progressing, despite my contribution.

I had started to enjoy some of the sexual opportunities offered in wartime London.

I remember making the acquaintance of a well dressed and attractive lady outside the Regent Palace Hotel near Piccadilly Circus. She invited me to accompany her to her home, which turned out to be in the outer suburbs. We took the tube and when we reached our destination a friendly police car, whose occupants were clearly familiar with the lady, drove us to her modest house. They waited outside, whilst we consummated the evening and then drove me back all the way to Hallam Street. When I tried to thank them, the police car driver replied: "That's all right, sir, we must all do our bit for the boys in blue."

Life in London was exciting and exhilarating.

The Americans had arrived in force and the Stage Door Canteen in Piccadilly had become my second home. I was involved in the opening night, where the tiny stage was graced with the presence of Fred Astaire, Bing Crosby and the host was Sir Anthony Eden. It was 1944.

My relationship with the film industry was growing through the continuing success of *March of the Movies*. I was, of course, closest to the British film industry and, in particular to J. Arthur Rank, the millionaire mill owner, who aspired to build from his Methodist background, a British owned film empire and Sir Alexander Korda, the Hungarian born genius, who, in my opinion, knew more about the business of making movies than anyone else outside of Hollywood. Korda was responsible for creating such masterpieces as

The Private Live of Henry VIII starring Charles Laughton, *The Scarlet Pimpernel* with Leslie Howard and *Fire Over England* starring Laurence Olivier.

At a private lunch at the Dorchester, which I helped organize for a few of the most important British producers, J. Arthur Rank and Sir Alexander Korda were the guests of honor. In a brief speech, Korda gave the best summary I have ever heard of the movie making business. With his strong Hungarian accent he reflected:

"When all is said and done, there are only four kinds of film. First, there are bad films, which lose money. Have nothing to do with them. Then there are bad films which make money. Some people make a career and a lot of money out of them" he added, looking straight at Herbert Wilcox. "Next there are good films which lose money; I have made some of them." We all thought of Charles Laughton in the magnificent, but financially unsuccessful *Rembrandt* and mentally bowed our heads.

"Finally," he concluded, "there are good films which make money,

Don't fool yourselves, there is no secret or magic formula enabling you to produce such films. However, should you be lucky enough to produce one, just go down on your knees to whatever God you worship and offer your grateful thanks."

Doesn't that say it all?

Another piece of advice I gained from Alexander Korda: "When in doubt about your next film—always announce John Bunyan's *Pilgrim's Progress*. The film was finally made in 1979 with Liam Neeson.

As for Hollywood, the program had brought me into contact with all the major Hollywood studios, particularly MGM, whose British management had hired me as a consultant. My mind was increasingly on the future.

For the Daily Mail, I had conceived the idea of the National Film Awards, determined by a popular vote and designed to be the British equivalent of the Oscars. The voting was to be encouraged and promoted by a Sunday broadcast show, in which the British stars would all appear in person in dramatization of scenes from the films they had made that year. The buzz bombs came down in London, but the war was about to end.

On D-Day in 1944, my ambition was to start traveling as soon as possible.

We celebrated the liberation of the Channel Islands with a gala broadcast, which I organized; but trouble of a different kind was brewing for me. My colleagues, particularly in the Army, had become jealous of my ability to combine my duties with the ORBS with my personal career. I found myself outvoted on the management committee and out of a job.

But I was still in the RAF and threatened with a posting to the Far East, where the war still continued. I sought the advice of a very experienced, non-commissioned officer in the RAF.

"Go sick" he advised me and I took his advice.

My mother's physician diagnosed me as suffering from exhaustion and I went without sleep for a few days. The friendly RAF lady physician, who was my psychiatrist, assured me that overwork had led to my physical condition and that, in her words: "I deserved and needed a rest."

Before Hiroshima and the end of the war in the Far East, I had received an honorable discharge from the RAF on medical grounds.

The only commercial air route to America was via Paris, where TWA was operating from a converted shop.

I arrived in New York, together with my partner from *March of the Movies*, Leslie Mitchell, who had pioneered transatlantic broadcasting, in a co-production with NBC, which he hosted together with NBC veteran, Ben Grauer.

I made my contacts with the radio industry, with particular attention to the successful entrepreneurs in the business of making and distributing transcribed program material, the business I aspired to enter on an International basis.

Chapter Two
My Journey Continues

And so - on to Hollywood.

As their new consultant, MGM looked after me in truly Royal fashion. I stayed in a suite in a mansion, just behind the Beverly Hills Hotel, which MGM maintained for visiting VIPs. They provided me with a chauffeur driven limo to visit the other studios.

In my first week in Hollywood, I met and interviewed Walt Disney, Cecil B, De Mille and Bing Crosby among others. On the subject of television, I found that I had more practical experience than my hosts. The BBC had commenced a daily television service from Alexandra Palace around 1937 and Leslie Mitchell, my host on *March of the Movies* was the first television announcer and highly publicized personality.

In 1946, America had a few experimental transmitters, including one located in an observatory in the hills overlooking Hollywood.

I found myself invited there to address a distinguished audience on the subject of the future of television.

In retrospect, it seems rather strange that a young British newcomer such as myself at that time should be asked and be able to accurately predict the shape of the giant which television in the USA was going to become. Back in London, my plans took shape.

Whist still a teenager, I had visualized the name Towers of London for my business and had already formed the parent company. I decided the best place to launch my International syndicated program business was Australia; where unlike the U.K., commercial broadcasting had a long and healthy history. But first, I needed programs to sell.

During my ORBS days I had already met and worked with Noël Coward. Coward had reopened the famous Theatre Royal in Drury Lane, which had been the war time headquarters of ENSA, with a new musical, *Pacific 1860* that had been the subject of unfavorable reviews.

Provided I used members of the cast, which included Graham Payn, Joyce Grenfell and the orchestra leader Mantovani in the program, Coward agreed to host and star in the thirteen programs of *The Noël Coward Show*, virtually an anthology of his own work.

Then I approached Gracie Fields, Britain's greatest vaudeville star, with an international reputation and she began a long association with me by recording, initially, thirteen programs of *The Gracie Fields Show*.

I conceived the idea of a drama anthology based on successful British films and with Anna Neagle as the star and Victoria the Great as the first subject; *London Playhouse* was launched.

I needed one more dramatic series and for this I thought of *Secret of Scotland Yard* and hired the one time Hollywood star Clive Brook, who was then living in London, as the narrator and host.

My package was complete and I set off for Australia.

C.G.Scrimgeour was a lay preacher and broadcaster who, after a spectacular row with the New Zealand Broadcasting Company, a BBC style monopoly, had moved to Australia.

With him as my advisor, I began my two week lightning assault on the Australian broadcasting establishment. I quickly sold *London Playhouse* to Paddy Campbell Jones, a new and enterprising Sydney based station proprietor and to the Macquarie Network, Australia's premier channel, the *Noël Coward* and *Gracie Fields* series.

In Melbourne, I had an introduction from Lord Rothermere, owner of the Daily Mail, to the legendary Australian newspaper tycoon, Sir Keith Murdoch, father of Rupert Murdoch, who owned the Melbourne Herald.

An interview did the trick and *Secrets of Scotland Yard* was sold to KGB, his Melbourne Station. The one thing I had to fear was action from the Australian unions to obstruct the upstart British invader. First, I guaranteed the overdraft of Australian Actors Equity and then signed a young but impressive Australian actor, Peter Finch, to direct a pilot episode for *The Sundowner*.

We recorded and sold the initial episode whilst I was still in Australia. To celebrate our success, we gave a reception to the media at the old Hotel Australia in Sidney, known to generations of Australians as "the pub." It was there that I learned, what I considered, the best of all the Australian tales I had heard.

Already, I had realized that the word "fucking" is a frequently expressible and indispensable part of the Australian vocabulary. There was, and probably still is, a small town in New South Wales called Coonawarra. No self respecting digger would call it anything other than "Coona-fucking-warra."

My tale concerns an Australian character, on loan from his origin in the North of England and known as a "winger." Our story begins in Sidney at the time of the outbreak of World War II.

Our storyteller, by chance, encounters an old friend, with the reputation of being a "winger," as he crosses the barracks square.

"How ya doing, Charlie?" he enquires?

"How am I fucking doing" the winger replies, "up and down the fucking barracks square from fucking morn to fucking night, with fucking sand in everything I fucking eat and fucking shit."

Our storyteller does not meet his friend again until early one morning aboard the liner the *Queen Mary*, which is conveying the first contingent of Australian troops to the Middle East.

"How ya doing, Charlie?" he enquires.

"How am I fucking doing?" is the response. "Up and down the fucking steps and wearing this fucking life jacket every fucking day and fucking night."

They do not see each other again until they collide in a shallow trench during the siege of Tobruk.

"How ya doing, Charlie?" he asks again.

"How am I fucking doing? Fucking sand wherever I fucking go," says the winger, but their conversation is interrupted and terminated by a direct hit from a German shell.

Their final encounter is on a cloud in heaven.

"Fancy meeting you here, Charlie. How ya doing?" is our story teller's welcome.

"How am I fucking doing? These fucking wings get in the fucking way of everything I fucking do. And look here's my fucking harp with only two fucking strings and a fucking matinee this afternoon."

So, until I returned for a regular series of annual visits, I bid Australia au revoir.

I made a weekend trip to New Zealand, where I also licensed our package of programs. I developed an affection for New Zealand and from then on, always spent a weekend there as the climax to my annual visits to Australia. In Wellington, like most visitors, I always stayed at the Royal Oak Hotel, a traditional English inn, run in a conservative style, reminiscent of a country town in the "home" country.

Tommy Trinder, who, in the post war years was almost as extensive a world traveler as myself, told me a tale of an engagement in Wellington, where he stayed at the Royal Oak in its only suite.

Each night, after he completed his stage appearance, when the hotel dining room was already closed, a cold collation was waiting for him in his suite. Each night too, he noted on duty the extremely attractive night receptionist, who gave him each evening an increasingly friendly smile. On his last night in town, Tommy took the plunge and invited the night receptionist up to his suite. She stayed until the morning.

Tommy, seized by a feeling of guilt, asked her whether she might be embarrassed if meeting any of her colleagues when leaving his room. "Oh, no" she replied with confidence. "I've never met the day staff."

From windy Wellington, I headed home. Back in London, I began a series of short, but regular visits to Paris. Some of the truly great, popular French stars crossed my path, including Maurice Chevalier, Edith Piaf, Simone Signoret, Charles Aznavour, who was to make a movie for me, and Yves Montand, whom I brought to London to entertain the guests at a Daily Mail National Film Award event.

I was stupid enough to open the bill with a popular sight act, The Bernard Brothers, which featured two noticeably camp male entertainers, in ballet frocks, who mimed the Andrews Sisters. They were, predictably, a riot, but during Yves Montand's debut, which followed, his songs in French, were accompanied by the conversations of the unimpressed guests. Yves Montand was not amused.

On another trip to Paris, I was accompanied by my lawyer, Jack Franks and a client, Reggie Hipwell, the founder and owner of a popular Forces Newspaper, Reveille. We were to meet a notorious character, who had spent the War Years in Monte Carlo and claimed to represent Radio Monte Carlo, which he told us was for sale. We met in his sumptuous apartment, lined with book cases full of authentic gold plate.

After dining, Reggie Hipwell, who had brought with him his ailing wife, who suffered from impaired vision, insisted on going out on the town. This was in the brief post war period before Martha Richard's edict closed down the bordellos for which Paris was justly famous. Whilst I stayed downstairs, keeping his wife company, Reggie went upstairs to sample the delights.

The 'Maison' we visited, was the notorious 122 Rue de Provence, which included, among its many attractions, the famous "Wagon Lit," which you could share with the lady of your choice, accompanied by the motions and sounds of a moving train.

I often returned to Paris, on my radio business, where I could count among my friends, Madame Billy, whose customers included the Prefect of Police, who provided the protection she required and Madame Claude, perhaps the greatest of all Parisian Madams. Her range of clients covered the whole international fields of fashion and finance and included many of the world's rich and famous and infamous.

Later, I wanted to film her life story and gathered together a great deal of material, but a low budget French production beat me to the punch—or pinch might be more appropriate.

It is, perhaps, not by chance that my recollection of the best bordello stories has myself in the role of a spectator and not, as an active participant.

My next story takes me many years forward in time to New York and an occasion in the not too distant past, before Mayor Giuliano's regime had cleaned up New York and swept into the past the many, no doubt mafia protected, apartments, mainly on the East side, which specialized in the world's oldest profession.

I was entertaining for dinner in New York an old friend from Spain, Andres Vicente Gomez, a notable producer and a partner on many occasions, which I shall later relate.

In delicate terms, he suggested that after dinner, as an infrequent visitor to New York, he would like to "see the town." We were old friends, so I had little difficulty in divining his meaning in "seeing the town." We adjourned to a nicely furnished split level apartment on the East side of town, with which I was familiar.

Whilst Andres sampled the delights which awaited upstairs, I, who it so happens, was more in the mood for conversation, had an amusing chat with a very attractive Puerto Rican novice. I have long noticed that most of the best stories in the world originate in New York. My longstanding New York attorney, Ed Rosenkrantz, usually relays the newest and best to me when we meet.

I entertained my Puerto Rican friend with some of these somewhat indelicate tales, culminating in, what my friends tell me, is one of the funniest stories they have ever heard.

It concerns the Pope, who discovers one morning in the Vatican that he is suffering from a most embarrassing condition—he has an erection, which will not go away.

He walks around during the day, holding his hands in front of him in a praying position, in order to conceal his predicament, but it requires an effort.

When, in the evening, he finally returns to his little private apartment in the Vatican, the best, if not only solution is to manually help himself. He is so occupied, that he does not hear the door click .There is a sudden, very bright flash of light. The Pope looks up, but as he does so, the door clicks shut.

The mystery is solved in the morning, when his personal mail includes a large brown envelope, hand delivered and marked for his special attention. It contains an enlarged stroboscopic shot of the Pope's hand in action on the offending portion of his anatomy, in which the unmistakable ring on the Pope's finger is clearly visible.

The still photo is accompanied by a typewritten note, in which the blackmailer threatens, that if he does not receive, in satisfactory form US$ 1,000,000 by midnight, he will sell the photo to *Hustler Magazine*.

There is an emergency meeting of the Vatican Council, who decide that there is no real alternative but to meet the blackmailer's demands. The money is raised from various confidential Vatican resources and, just before midnight, in pouring rain, the Pope's private secretary ventures outside Saint Peter's to make the exchange.

He returns with another large envelope. The blackmailer has kept his side of the bargain, for the envelope contains, what the blackmailer swears to be the original negative and the tiny little Japanese camera with which the shot was taken. The Pope is vastly relieved but overwhelmed with guilt.

He goes to his own priest, who suggests some form of penance. For the next six months, the Pope must wear the little Japanese, miniature camera on a chain around his neck.

The months go by, until one day during the Pope's weekly audience, when he greets visiting pilgrims to Rome, the Pope is confronted by the presence of fifty Japanese Catholics.

At the end of the audience the fifty pilgrims are, as tradition permits, allowed to file past the Pope and, one by one, receive his blessing and kiss the Pope's hand which wears the Papal Ring.

The last of the Japanese pilgrims looks up to the Pope and spots the camera.

"Ah," he declares "you have little Japanese camera."

The Pope nods his head.

"How much you pay" the pilgrim asks.

"One million dollars" the Pope whispers.

"Oh," observes the Japanese pilgrim. "Someone see you coming."

My Puerto Rican listener thoroughly enjoyed this and other stories, originating from the same source.

Some months later, Ed dined with me. I sensed he might be having some temporary marital problems, when he suggested that we should go out on the town. We adjourned to the same East side apartment, where Ed spotted my attractive and now more experienced Puerto Rican friend. He invited her upstairs, whilst I exchanged some amusing reminiscences with the madam. Later, when Ed returned from upstairs with his new friend, I asked her whether she had enjoyed herself. "Oh," she replied, "your friend is very nice, but I do wish he didn't keep telling me this old Pope story."

It was quite some time before Ed forgave me.

It's also now my turn to apologize for the digression.

My next overseas trip was to South Africa. My friends from IBC, Frank Lamping and his boss Richard Meyer, operated a pirate radio station in Lourenco Marques, and helped me to wrap up this market. I went on, via Dakar, to South America.

We landed, first in Recife, where my first night in Brazil coincided with a local election, with the victor riding through the town square firing a loaded pistol to celebrate. Next came Rio de Janeiro, where I made friends that were to later serve me as a film producer. In Buenos Aires, Argentina, I was the guest of the Peronistas and, in the apartment of Yankalevich, the radio impresario who discovered Evita Peron. I was invited to organize an international radio service, "The Voice of Peron."

I was intrigued, but declined. I had plenty of work awaiting me in London.

But first came a labor of love. Noël Coward was chairman of the Actors Orphanage, a traditional appointment occupied by the person, generally considered to be, at the top of his profession.

Before the war, the Theatrical Garden Party, always held in Regent's Park, was one of the events of the London season and provided, from its profit, the principal financial support for the Orphanage. After the war the Crown Commissioners had decided they would not continue to make Regent's Park available. Noël had arranged, as a substitute, to utilize the Polo Grounds at Hurlingham. I went about the task with energy and enthusiasm.

I signed up with the contractors for Royal Ascot to provide all the tents, marquees and other furnishings required. I mobilized all my contacts for providing new and original ideas, including a circus with Rex Harrison as the ringmaster. Finally, the great day, traditionally a Saturday, arrived and Fred Wilby, an outstanding stage manager who worked for me, arrived in a limo to pick me up and take me to Hurlingham.

On the way, I mused with Fred about how much I had already achieved at such an early age and it seemed, that the only event I had, so far, not staged was a water spectacle.

Fred opened the window—it had started to rain.

"Harry," Fred said "it looks like you have a water spectacle on your hands today."

I looked out the window and indeed it poured and poured and poured all day.

At the end of the afternoon, I was summoned by "the Master," as Noël Coward was known as in the profession, to his personal marquee.

The "Master" lay prostrate, his head on the lap of the Duchess of Kent, whilst Richard Attenborough, now Lord Attenborough, massaged his feet. The partners from the accountancy firm Price Waterhouse read out the results. Far from providing for the orphans, the Theatrical Garden Party had lost a substantial sum of money. The "Master" was, as always, gracious.

"Harry," he said, "I am not blaming you personally, but hence forth, the three bloodiest words in the English language are: Theatrical. Garden. Party."

I slunk away.

On Monday, I reported the results to Lord Rothermere, proprietor of the Daily Mail. "How much will it cost to keep the orphans for a year" was his only comment as he reached for his cheque book.

I rushed around to Noël's apartment in Gerard Road, Victoria, and handed him the cheque. He examined it carefully and, again graciously, acknowledged the generous gift. "My dear Harry" he said, "you have truly redeemed yourself."

Out of a multitude of Noël Coward stories, I most appreciate and recall two more.

In the early days of the war, Noël, seeking a useful way of helping the war effort, went to Australia to make a series of patriotic broadcasts. Returning to his hotel in Sidney on a Saturday night, after dining with the Governor General, he was accosted, alone, in the elevator by a drunken digger.

"I know who you are" slurred the drunk, "you're Mr. fucking Noël Coward come to tell us Australians on how to win the fucking war. You've been here for four fucking weeks now, say something Australian."

Noël, adjusting his bow tie as he stepped out of the elevator, replied "Kangaroo."

In London for the Coronation, Noël was, together with a friend, Joyce Carey, watching, from a stand, the procession of guests, as they drove in carriages back from the ceremony in Westminster Abbey.

The procession had been arranged so that Commonwealth dignitaries shared the same carriage.

It poured with rain.

Queen Salote of Tonga, riding in an open carriage, won the cheers of the crowd as she stood upright and, ignoring the rain, waved in acknowledgement to their cheers. Seated next to her was an inconspicuous small man in a dress suit, who was actually the Sultan of Zanzibar.

"Who's he?" enquired Joyce, as she studied her program without success,

"Probably her lunch," Noël replied.

Soon I was back in New York and paying my first visit to Canada. There, I succeeded in making my initial program sale in North America, *London Playhouse* to Imperial Oil.

Mother had joined me in New York, where I rented an unfurnished apartment at the Hotel Meurice, which I promptly furnished from Bloomingdales in thirty minutes. Opportunity was again waiting for me back in London.

Radio Luxembourg, after its war time role as an instrument of Nazi propaganda, was back on the air with the support of international advertisers, who needed English language programming with appeal in the U.K. I jumped aboard the bandwagon and my catalogue of programs grew at an amazing rate.

Soon I had over a score of different series in production in London.

They included musical programs with Gracie Fields, Vera Lynn, Edmondo Ross, Donald Peers, Charlie Kunz, Anne Ziegler and Webster Booth and the Keynotes. My dramatic series included *The London Story* starring John Mills, a serialization of J. B. Priestley's *The Good Companions* starring Wilfred Pickles, a crime story *Fabian of the Yard* and a twenty six episode, all star, version of J.B. Priestley's *The Good Companions* starring Wilfred Pickles as Jess Oakroyd and Petula Clark as Suzie Dean.

I sold this series to Cadbury's Chocolate.

But soon I had another client, Bovril, who wanted a quarter hour series. My first target was the Radio Doctor, who became famous in Labour circles for his remark "that it was penicillin not politicians who improved the health of the British people,"

The Radio Doctor declined my offer on the grounds that in view of his position on the Medical Board. It would be unethical to accept my offer.

Years later, when he was Post Master General, and I headed the ATV delegation seeking to be a Program Contractor for commercial television, he greeted me with the remark, "You tried to buy me for commercial broadcasting. Now, you're trying to sell me to ATV as being a competent Program Contractor for commercial television."

Back to J.B. Priestley.

His wartime *Postscripts* after the nine o'clock news had made him, next to Winston Churchill, the biggest booster of the nation's morale.

Priestley agreed to record a new series of twenty six *Postscripts* for me, which I immediately sold to Bovril.

Every week I used to visit him at his apartment at the Albany in Piccadilly, a famous abode of writers from Lord Byron to Terence Rattigan, and he would hand me his weekly "Postscript."

I felt very proud.

My young people's programs were headed by the long running and popular series *Dan Dare – Pilot of the Future*. My talk programs included the series of postscripts by J. B. Priestley and Sir Thomas Beecham, as a classical disk jockey.

My father had had a long association with Sir Thomas Beecham, which started when my father was the house manager of London's Covent Garden Opera House during the memorable season of, I believe, 1911, when for the first time, Beecham brought such great Russian opera singers as Feodor Chaliapin to the West.

Among my father's duties as house manager, was to go and see Chaliapin in his dressing room, every night before his appearance and lay out one hundred golden sovereigns on the table. Then—and only then—would Chaliapin start to put on his make-up.

Thus the custom was born and followed vigorously by every Hollywood agent to have a star's remuneration put into escrow at least seven days before reporting to work.

Back to Sir Thomas Beecham.

There are a fund of stories concerning Beecham's wit and sometimes savage sense of humor. One of my favorite stories concerns his visit to Australia, where he had been invited to conduct the symphony orchestras of Melbourne and Sydney. When confronted with the magnificent view of the famous Sydney Harbor Bridge, Beecham was asked, "There, what about that, Sir Thomas?"

His response was, "I don't like it. Can't you have it removed?"

When Sir Thomas worked for me, we started the recordings at eleven o'clock in the morning. I, personally and dutifully, brought him a glass of ginger beer, a poor substitute for champagne, which he preferred on other occasions. Sir Thomas was very gracious and added a sample of his devastating wit to every program.

My variety series included *Much Binding in the Marsh*, which I took back from the BBC and, once again, made the headlines in the U.K. and Australia and a variety series recorded every Sunday on the stage of the London Palladium.

Concerning *Much Binding in the Marsh*, it had its BBC birthplace in a weekly series entitled *Mediterranean Merry-Go-Round* that provided in turn, shows by the three armed forces, the R.A.F., the Army and the Royal navy, who contributed *The Navy Lark*.

The latter starred a comedian, Eric Barker, who was married to a rather dominant wife, Pearl Hackney. Whilst I had been demobilized between VE day and the surrender of Japan, Eric was still in the Navy, with the prospect of being sent to the Pacific. I, somewhat unkindly, observed that he was "torn between Pearl Hackney and Pearl Harbor."

During the war, Eric found himself invited to a party in the Officer's Mess of a nearby station, forming part of the Royal Naval Air Force. One of its war time officers was Ralph Richardson. During a general conversation Richardson remarked that the all important element in any film script were the last lines.

"I quite agree," piped up Eric Barker, the first time he had spoken at the gathering.

"Quiet, Eric," whispered his wife, Pearl Hackney. "You have never been in a film."

"Oh yes, I have," responded Eric, "and I agree."

"What were the last lines?" Richardson diplomatically enquired.

Eric responded, "Drink Cadbury's Chocolate."

I used another series from the BBC *Twenty Questions* and brought back Stewart Macpherson from Canada as the host. I signed up all the available talent and quickly offered the only alternative to the BBC to British radio performers. I did not miss any opportunity to make the business a two way trade.

In Ireland, I made a deal with the famous Abbey Theatre in Dublin and persuaded Barry Fitzgerald to act as the host. For the initial program we chose Lady Gregory's *Spreading the News*. After spending a week in Dublin, securing the actors, who had all acquired London agents, we finally assembled the cast on the stage at the Abbey Theatre, rehearsed and broke for lunch at the neighboring pub.

From the window, I happened to see our star, Mae Craig, leaving through the stage door with a shopping bag and boarding a tram. When I enquired about the reason I was told, "Ah, it's a Friday and on Fridays Mae always visits her husband's grave." We waited three hours, consoled ourselves with Guinness and finally recorded the show.

I took Stanley Holloway, Eliza's father of *My Fair Lady* fame, to Australia and New Zealand on a concert tour and to record a radio series with Australian talent. We had many joyous times together.

James Mason, the British actor, had arrived in New York for the first time, but owing to a contractual dispute, could not work in the States. I persuaded him to come to Toronto and, over an intensive two week period, record twelve episodes for the *London Playhouse* series, with a supporting cast of Canadian actors.

I still had to find a way of breaking into, by far the most important market, the United States.

I had observed that the Frederic W. Ziv Company, which I represented overseas, was attracting major movie stars, who for health or other reasons were attracted to the comparative comfort of a recording studio, to sign up for syndicated series. Diverting for a moment to a story told me by Herb Golden, head of talent acquisitions at the Ziv Company.

One day, he received a call from Ray Stark, an agent who was later to have a long and illustrious career, who made him an offer: "We own the rights on C. S. Forrester's *Horatio Hornblower*. We can get you Gregory Peck for a television series."

Herb Golden's response: "You're a liar Ray Stark. You always have been and you always will be; Harry Towers controls the *Horatio Hornblower* rights. He has the series on the CBS Network, starring Michael Redgrave."

Ray Stark's immediate reply, "In that case, we'll get you Gregory Peck in something else."

Now back to the Ziv Company and their acquisition of major talent. Their latest conquest was Humphrey Bogart and Lauren Bacall. I had a contract with Orson Welles, who had just appeared as Harry Lime in the movie *The Third Man*.

I had first met Orson through Fletcher Markle, a Canadian Radio and TV director, who had worked for Orson, directing a summer series of his Mercury Theatre in 1946. It was Fletcher who first introduced me to Orson, when we met at a screening theatre at Columbia Studios. Also present were Harry Cohn, the owner of Columbia Studios and Rita Hayworth, then Orson's wife and probably the most glamorous woman in the word at that time. They were looking at a cut of *The Lady From Shanghai*, that Orson had directed and in which he co-starred with Rita Hayworth. How the film got financed and made was a story in itself.

After Mike Todd pulled out, Orson had been touring the provincial towns of North America with his version of Jules Verne's *Around the World in 80 Days* which included a scene with Orson, as a hypnotist, cutting a lady in half. The lady was Rita Hayworth.

Orson was desperately short of money and couldn't meet his weekly payroll. So, he called Harry Cohn from the stage door keeper's office of the theatre in which he was appearing. Orson offered Harry the opportunity to be involved in a film which Orson would direct, starring Rita Hayworth and himself, provided Harry could transfer the more than fifty thousand dollars he needed so urgently.

Harry Cohn was interested, but wanted to know the title of the project. Orson looked around and saw a paperback copy of the "Lady of Shanghai," which Orson had never heard of before. Nevertheless he gave the title to Harry and praised it very highly. Harry Cohen sent Orson the money and then bought the film rights to the book. Orson met the payroll and the film was made, but bore little resemblance to the book, save the title.

I had learned from Alexander Korda, the story of how Orson, who later confirmed the tale to me, had, at first reluctantly, accepted the role of Harry Lime. Korda, who had brought David O. Selznick into the deal as a financial partner, was en route to New York, with a brief overnight stop in Rome.

Orson, who already had the reputation of being a difficult man, was in Europe for tax reasons. He had made a string of movies for Twentieth Century Fox, with whom his price per film was US$ 100,000. Korda, for the role of Harry Lime, could not afford more than US$ 50,000.

He knew, that if he failed to convince Orson, Selznick would insist that he hire his choice, Noël Coward, who Korda was convinced was absolutely wrong for Harry Lime. Korda met with Orson in his suite at the Grand Hotel in Rome and pleaded with him to accept the role at the reduced fee.

Orson refused and Korda, as he was just about to leave, picked up his expensive overcoat, which had a massive tear from being damaged on the aircraft gangway when he arrived. He threw the overcoat at Orson's feet and declared, "Here I am, offering you the second best part of your life, after *Citizen Kane* and I, the producer, can't even afford a new overcoat."

Orson's response was immediate, "Alright—I'll do it for US$ 50,000."

When I first viewed *The Third Man*, I already knew that Orson was broke and needed money to complete the post production of his version of *Othello* that enjoyed the unique distinction of having four different actresses, all clearly visible, in the role of Desdemona. I recognized that Harry Lime could form a wonderful basis for a radio series.

I knew that my literary agent, David Higham, also represented Graham Greene, the author of *The Third Man*.

I asked him whether his contract with Korda covered character rights. Initially, David was not completely clear about the definition of such rights, but after checking he was able to satisfy me and I acquired the rights for a radio series. I then checked with the music publisher, Chappell's, to ensure that I could obtain a license to use *The Third Man* theme for a radio series. I brought Anton Karas to London to record on his zither the famous theme and also a complete series of cues to provide the score of the radio series.

In that same Grand Hotel suite in Rome, where Korda met Orson, I signed a deal with Orson for fifty two episodes in *The Lives of Harry Lime*. Two weeks later, in London, Orson stepped up to the microphone; as the sound of a pistol shot interrupted the zither performance of Anton Karas and, for the first time, uttered the words, "This was the shot that killed Harry Lime. He died in a sewer beneath Vienna, but before he died he lived many lives. Let me tell you about just one of them. How come I know so much? Because my name—is Harry Lime."

Korda and Selznick were furious.

I met with Korda, who admitted that he could not contest our rights. I also gained a friend, his truly wonderful attorney, Tristram Owen, who offered to become my solicitor. We worked together for many years until he retired. On one occasion, some years later, I arrived, with Tristram, in the Manager's office of the Bank of America, in the West End of London, on a Friday afternoon in August, an hour before the bank closed. Tristram plunked down the battered briefcase, he always carried, on the manager's desk and announced, "I don't know what your plans are for the weekend, but we intend to make a movie." Remember, that although this was the Bank of America, we were in London and it was August.

We booked the manager and the assistant manager into Claridges Hotel, which was nearby and closed on Sunday afternoon. What a lawyer!—What a man!—I miss him greatly.

At that time my output included a drama series *The Queen's Men*. Each program commenced with the martial music of the Royal Canadian Mounted Police (RCMP) March Past. Then in every program the music was overlaid by the voice of Lorne Greene, Canada's Number One broadcaster, saying: "The Queen's Men—the true stories of the men and women who, for over a hundred years have kept the Queen's Peace in Canada."

The series had been broadcast successfully worldwide, before it was pointed out to me that the misspelling of one word in the above sentence could lead to an unfortunate "double entendre." Hey Ho.

Chapter Three
A Diverson: The Night Life in London

Back, when I first moved into a London apartment, I had also given a thought to getting a country retreat. First, I rented a country cottage, in Telscombe, near Lewis, on the Brighton line. The Squire of Telscombe, was Ernest Thornton Smith, who with his brother owned the famous department store, Fortnum & Mason in London's Piccadilly.

By chance, I was in Telscombe and met Garfield Western, the Canadian born entrepreneur. It was Garfield who bought from Ernest Fortnum and Mason, which still, to this day, remains the property of Garfield Western's family.

My father spent more and more time in Telscombe and, later on, made it his home. My mother, used to be driven down to Telscombe on Friday afternoon(s) and back again to London on Monday, where she spent the rest of the week. Thus, I had to share my London apartment with my mother, for the whole of the week. I needed some change of scenery to enable me to complete my ever increasing work load.

It was then, that I developed the habit, of visiting night clubs, where I could develop new ideas, making the necessary notes.

I always started my evening at Percival Murray's Cabaret Club. This was perhaps the most famous spot in London. It was, notably, the place where Christine Keeler and Mandy Rice Davies had worked, who were principal players in the Profumo affair, which ultimately helped to bring down Harold MacMillan's conservative British government.

I knew the club well. It was quite small and intimate, with a tiny stage and a very small, resident band. There were about thirty five attractive girls in the stage show. They were so short of space that the girls had to use a store across the street for make up and wardrobe changes.

The first girl I ever picked up in Murray's, was Doro George. She was Anglo Indian or Anglo Burmese; an incredibly beautiful woman and great fun. We became friends and Doro was my frequent dinner companion.

Percival Murray had a very smart trick. There were three cubicles at the back of the cabaret club which were wired for sound. When Murray, or his cohorts, saw anybody of potentially dubious reputation, they took them directly to one of the wired cubicles. Murray was in constant contact with Scotland Yard. They valued the information that he could give them a great deal. Like all night clubs, of any era, they had bouncers to get rid of "undesirables." Murray's had the greatest bouncers of any club I had ever seen. The slightest sign of trouble and the perpetrators were moved off the premises so quickly one hardly knew they had left.

Murray, himself, used to tour the provinces and scout for talented, young girls, who wanted theatrical experience in London. Obviously, Murray never hired anyone under the age of eighteen, but the closer to eighteen the better. Murray gave them a contract, brought them to London and put them up in a small, but comfortable hotel in Soho.

After about a month, the new girls would start to share a room with another, more experienced, girl from the club. Often, there were ladies selling very expensive jewelry and clothing, such as mink coats, all on the installment basis. Murray reckoned that after about a month of working at the club, the young lady herself would be interested in shall we say, extending her income.

However, Murray was very adamant that the girls could never leave the club with a customer. So the ladies who wanted to extend their income would meet their "new friends" at Lawley's, the hardware store just down the road on Regent's Street. So much for Percival Murray.

The second place I used to like to visit was the Embassy Club on Bond Street, a very distinguished and refined night spot. I felt rather special that the seat I normally occupied had, in the old days, been reserved for the Duke of Windsor, before the abdication. Lew and his brother and partner Leslie Grade used to book the chorus line at the Embassy.

Michael Grade, Leslie Grade's son came to be chairman of the board of Governors at the BBC, before quitting the job to take up the same post with their competitors, ITV.

Although there were ladies of the evening present, they used to be seated in a certain section of the club, so they wouldn't be confused with the paying guests. In a way, the ladies were guests too, but they didn't have to pay for anything themselves. It was the club patrons who would look after that side of the business. First requirement was, of course, a bottle of champagne.

Once, around about this period, I was on a flight from New York back to London and found myself sitting next to a very attractive young lady who seemed rather familiar.

My mother met me at London airport and we all took the car back to our apartment and I dropped the young lady off on the way. After saying good bye, I suddenly realized that it was the normally scantily clad cigarette girl from the Embassy Club. I hadn't recognized her right away, due to the fact that I had never seen her in her street clothes, nor in broad daylight.

Quite late, one evening, I was coming out of the Embassy Club, when Bulganin and Khrushchev were in town. Khrushchev was the first Russian Head of State to visit a western city. Their arrival was a big event. After dinner at Downing Street the motorcade was on their way back, from   Piccadilly coming up Bond Street As soon as a number of the girls caught sight of the Rolls Royce, with a motor cycle escort, they opened their little hand bags and pulled out lace hankies and waved enthusiastically.

This was in the days before the legislation forbade street prostitution in London and this was a period when many girls still plied their trade on Bond Street. They were mostly French girls, who had married British men, so that they couldn't be deported.

Khrushchev looked thrilled and waved back. This was his first opportunity, in London, to meet the "proletariat." The event was very entertaining. There was nobody from the press there and, as far as I know, I am the first person telling this story.

The Russian delegation was living at Claridges, mother's and my favorite hotel. Whenever I was in London, mother and I used to have Sunday brunch at the lovely lounge restaurant, the Causerie, which, sadly, is no more. This time I noticed that there was intense security in the lobby; things had been moved around and I recognized a couple of Scotland Yard officers. As I knew the hotel's concierge, George, quite well, I asked him, discretely, for the reason of all this excitement. "Well, sir, he replied, Mr. Khrushchev and Mr. Bulganin have taken the whole of the first floor and it would be simply dreadful, if they were to be assassinated on the premises."

Talking of Heads of State; I remember, being in the hotel on the weekend of the Coronation of the present Queen. Again, there was a lot of commotion and heavy security. This time George explained, "We have five kings staying at the hotel tonight." These were the last five kings in Europe.

Now, on to the third club, which was the Astor Club just off Berkley Square, where "the Nightingale sang." The Astor was a club of a very different kind. I always used to call it the "gangster club" because a percentage of the regular customers were clearly of the criminal profession. If you saw a large party it was a coming out party not necessarily a coming out of a junior member but a coming out of prison party.

The club had an atmosphere of its own, which was very special. To really enjoy it you had to realize that this was a cabaret which was in tune with the majority of the customers, Tommy Trinder used to sing 'Just Because I'm a Londoner' and when everyone joined in, you had the heart of London.

Sadly, I last met Tommy very much later in his life, when I was in, of all places, Zimbabwe. I was coming out of my hotel and asked the concierge if he could recommend some place I could get a drink with a nice atmosphere. He recommended a Japanese owned club not far from the hotel where they had a line of chorus girls scantily dressed and one act Tommy Trinder. Tommy met me in the bar and we talked about old times, old friends and some very old secrets.

As we were about to go, I said, "Look after yourself, Tommy, what are your plans?"

"Well," he replied. "I am going from here to Toronto to appear on a show called *Those Were the Days*, then I am entertaining Her Majesty Forces in Germany for four weeks and then I am booked for pantomime at Eastbourne."

I felt that that was so indicative of his professional approach to life, that I have never forgotten it.

The Stork Club, which still exists on Swallow Street, was another favorite of mine. It was the perfect place to pick up female company, if you wanted to. I remember meeting a journalist there, who specialized in exposés of a sexual nature; any sex scandals in London were his specialty. He had a standard formula for closing his interviews saying, "She offered me sex in exchange for money and I made an excuse and left." I have often thought that he might make up a book composed entirely of these excuses.

On one occasion, when I was rather bored, I went to a night club, the name of which I cannot remember. It was managed by two Italians and I knew it mainly because of the maitre d', Pip. I had known Pip from an earlier period at the Astor Club. I went in, late one Saturday night, and the young ladies who where looking for customers had all been booked out.

In the cabaret, they featured a young pretty girl, who did an acrobatic act with, what looked like, large rolls of linoleum. They must have been quite light, because she had four of them and she would balance them on her feet, while lying on the floor.

When I had paid my bill and was ready to go Pip said: "You looking for company this evening, Mr. Towers?" When I showed interest he told me, that the young lady, who had just performed that acrobatic act, was looking for a bit of extra money.

Well I met her and took her back to my apartment. I'm very glad to say she did not place me on her feet and balance me up in the air, as she had done with the rolls of linoleum. We were much more conventional in our enjoyable, physical activities.

So much for the night clubs of London.

One of my favorite cabaret entertainers was Beatrice Lilly. To hear her sing "You're a fraud Maud" or "There are Fairies at the Bottom of the Garden" with her incomparable wit and style was a truly enjoyable experience.

Beatrice's one woman show "An Evening with Beatrice Lilly" had a twelve months run on Broadway with ecstatic reviews from the sometimes vicious New York theatre critics. One year later a Canadian singer with more money than talent hired a Broadway theatre for her own one woman show. The reviews in the next day's paper were scathing including one which described the performance as "An evening without Beatrice Lilly."

Here is another example of the power of the New York theatre critics; John Van Druten's play *I Am A Camera* was the inspiration for the musical *Cabaret* it was greeted with a two word review "No Leica."

The prolific New York stage producer David Merrick thought he had a solution for the problem of the "bad reviews." He found a group of individuals who just happened to have the same name as the major theatre critics. With their identical names prominently displayed in the advertising campaign that covered the New York subway system the phony reviews were full of praise for David Merrick's new productions.

The people using the subway and seeing the ads soon became suspicious, being aware of the different reviews in the newspapers.

So David Merrick abandoned the idea.

At Sardis, the New York restaurant where the actors directly involved in a new Broadway show were eagerly awaiting the delivery of the first edition of the morning papers to see how they fared, the evening could go two ways. If the review was favorable it was champagne all the way. If the reviews were unfavorable one could hear a pin drop and the place often became a "cemetery of dreams."

In the United States, MGM had decided to enter the transcription business and speedily developed a program of radio series, utilizing their contract stars and properties. I became their overseas sales agent.

When they made a deal with the Mutual Network in the US for their entire program, I contributed two series: *The Lives of Harry Lime* and a new version of *The Gracie Fields Show*, featuring a Canadian host I had adopted and imported, Bernard Braden. But Selznick, who still had considerable influence at MGM, objected.

A Diversion: The Night Life in London

I picked up the tapes from the MGM headquarters in New York and took them over to ABC (American Broadcasting Company), where we made a syndicated deal. MGM had contracted with Mutual to provide them with an Orson Welles series and they turned to me for help.

I remembered my *Secrets of Scotland Yard* series and revived and reworked it under the new title *The Black Museum*. Orson, who needed money as usual, had just opened his stage version of *Othello* at the St. James Theatre. A particularly vicious London critic, the Canadian, Milton Shulman, had given an unfavorable review under the headline "Citizen Coon."

I picked up Orson at the stage door on the second night of the play. In the taxi, I handed him the contract for fifty two episodes for *The Black Museum*.

Orson signed the contract, with the remark: "The things I do for money."

The series is, to this day, still being successfully broadcast.

My success with the two series with Orson had opened other doors to me in the United States. Whilst television was growing fast, the networks were struggling to maintain their existing radio operations and needed programming, delivering international stars at a reasonable price.

My next customer was CBS (Columbia Broadcasting System), where I sold a series of fifty two adventures of C.S. Forrester's *Horatio Hornblower* starring, Michael Redgrave.

Orson suggested to me a series on Baroness Orczy's *The Scarlet Pimpernel*.

I checked to learn that the Baroness had written a sequel *The Adventures of the Scarlet Pimpernel*, to which the rights were available. I signed Marius Goring for the lead and sold the series to NBC (National Broadcasting Company).

This time, I made peace with Korda and gave him a share of the profits.

There was still one literary classic available, Sir Arthur Conan Doyle's *Sherlock Holmes*. I cleared the rights with his sons and looked for the perfect cast.

I persuaded Sir John Gielgud to portray Holmes and for Dr. Watson I chose Sir Ralph Richardson. For sixteen weeks we met, first at the studios I rented in Portland Place, for a morning rehearsal. Then we went for lunch to the Etoile Restaurant on Charlotte Street, and back again to the studios in Portland Place to record the program.

On the definitive episode *The Empty House* that introduced Conan Doyle's Emperor of Crime, the unforgettable Professor Moriarty, I decided a special guest was required.

Orson was in Paris but I convinced him to come over on the boat train for one day. I met him at Victoria Station and told him the schedule. At the mention of the word "rehearsal," he exploded. "In radio," he declared "an artist does not rehearse. He just performs and gets paid."

Orson had never met Gielgud and Richardson and, when he arrived at the recording studios, Ralph Richardson was already there, underlining his script in blue and red pencil. "What is he doing?" Orson whispered to me.

"He's underlining his lines in blue and the cue lines in red" I explained.

Orson sat down next to Ralph, introduced himself and asked if he could borrow his pencils.

We all went to our usual rendezvous for lunch and the conversation between my three guests was as amusing and wonderful as I have ever enjoyed. When asked by Gielgud about his future plans, Orson responded with the news that he planned to play Shakespeare's *King Lear* on stage.

Gielgud's response: "Not in London I hope."

We returned to record the program, still a fondly remembered classic to this day on CD. As Orson departed for Paris, Ralph Richardson benignly observed, "What a charming young man. I don't believe all those stories about him."

My customers for this and other series included the BBC. My final conquest was Lord Laurence Olivier, whom I persuaded to host and star in an anthology series *Theatre Royal*.

My customer was again NBC, now in the personage of its new and aggressive boss, Ted Cott.

Ted came to England for his honeymoon. Laurence Olivier was happily not available in London at that time to meet Mr. Cott. Ted, on his departure, entrusted me with the task of giving his greetings to: "Laurence Oliver and Lady Lay," which, needless to say, I did.

The other day I found myself watching on television Alfred Hitchcock's masterpiece, the original *The Thirty Nine Steps*, with its exciting finale in the London Palladium, a theatre I know so well. I was captivated by the charm of its hero, portrayed by Robert Donat, a British actor who went to Hollywood, but returned to London to play the title role in *Goodbye Mr. Chips*.

I met him one day in the studio in Portland Place, where I recorded so many of my classic transcription programs. Robert Donat, in his later years, suffered badly from asthma and was uninsurable. He had consented, as a personal favour, to record a radio version of one of his movies. I forget the name of the movie but it concerned a titled British gentleman who owns his ancestral castle, but is in the process of selling it to an American millionaire. Half way through the recording session, Robert Donat suffered a bad attack of asthma, and we had to break for an hour, whilst we waited for him to recover.

When the recording was completed, Robert Donat apologized to me for causing the delay, and gave his good wishes and thanks to the supporting cast and recording crew. He was indeed a fine gentleman, and I am proud to have met him.

Chapter Four
New York, New York
– and Elsewhere

In these heady radio days, I continued to maintain two homes, or three, if I include our country cottage in Telscombe, near Brighton. The first home was in Hallam Street and the second in New York on West 58th Street.

As a child, when during the summer my father managed a touring production, we spent every weekend touring from one provincial town to another. Now, I maintained this habit, but, instead, commuted between London and New York.

I nearly always traveled on British Airways and shared the frequent flyer record between London and New York with Harry Winston, the jeweler. In the pre-jet days, one needed to make two stops for refueling purposes, on the transatlantic route.

Flying East to West, the first stop was at Shannon in Ireland, which had developed into one of the busiest airports in the world and the second stop was one of two alternatives, Gander in Newfoundland or Goose Bay in Labrador, both developed during the war.

I first learned of the advent of a new and exciting means of travel, the Boeing Strato-cruiser from a very experienced source, Captain Kelly Rogers of BOAC, who had been Sir Winston Churchill's pilot during his war time years, pioneering transatlantic journeys. On one occasion, we found ourselves marooned together at Shannon, surrounded by American Airlines passengers, delayed in Shannon by a pilot's strike.

We hired a car and driver to take us to Dublin. En route to the city we stopped at every pub we encountered, so that Captain Rogers could "keep up his spirits."

Thus, I was told that the Boeing Strato-cruiser would carry on its small upper deck a bar, to offer refreshments to the First Class passengers. Needless to say, I enjoyed the upper deck. It made the trips feel so much shorter.

On one occasion, two of my fellow passengers, were Trevor Howard, notorious for his like of "strong spirits" and Herbert Wilcox, husband of Anna Neagle, who had produced Howard's most recent film *Cockleshell Heroes*.

They had been on a tour of the United States to publicize the film. I met them in New York at the famous Little Club, run by its popular proprietor, Billy Little. I noticed some scaffolding at the back of the club and assumed that Billy was enlarging the premises. "Oh no," declared Billy, who was no fool. "We're making the club smaller."

Trevor was in a very happy condition when we boarded the flight. I don't believe he heard the Captain's announcement that, due to bad weather conditions, we were making an emergency stopover in Monkton, New Brunswick. It was close to midnight, on a Sunday, when an extremely inebriated Trevor demanded, from the girl behind the counter in the airport coffee shop, "a double scotch."

When he failed to get what he wanted, to the extreme embarrassment of Herbert Wilcox, Trevor burst through the doors of the coffee shop and ran onto the tarmac. He mistakenly believed we were still in New York and were in danger of missing our flight.

"Taxi, taxi," he shouted, before falling flat down on the tarmac, unconscious.

Another memory of Herbert Wilcox and his wife, Anna Neagle. One Christmas season, Anna starred in the annual revival of James Barry's *Peter Pan*. At the Piccadilly Theatre, that mistress of impersonation, Florence Desmond, was in the cast of a successful revue. As the finale, Florence appeared in the full regalia of an aging Queen Victoria.

She slowly advanced to the centre of the stage to the music of Edward Elgar's "Pomp and Circumstance." When she reached the centre stage, the music stopped. And so did she. She whispered into the microphone; "If only Albert could see me playing Peter Pan."

Some years later, Herbert Wilcox had the misfortune to go bankrupt.

He had been a long time member of that elite theatrical establishment, the Garrick Club, which had a club rule, that required the expulsion of any bankrupt member. Anna Neagle appeared personally before the Club Committee and pleaded that in his case the rule should be waived. She succeeded, and Herbert Wilcox remained a member of the Garrick Club for the rest of his life.

The standard routine on BOAC flights was that the First Class passengers would retire upstairs to the lounge, whilst the crew converted their seats into proper sleeping berths. The more drink happy of the passengers didn't bother to come back downstairs.

Another time, again due to weather conditions, I had to spend the night in Montreal. The director Byron Haskins, another notorious alcoholic, lay drunk on the floor of the lounge and was overlooked, as the rest of the passengers and crew disembarked. Byron woke up in the freezing and empty aircraft, parked in a hangar. He imagined he was dead.

Finally, Byron's beating on the sides of the aircraft gained the attention of a night watchman, who thought the plane was haunted and ran away. A half frozen Byron was rescued and emerged from the plane.

Meantime, I'd made friends with a fellow traveler, an American divorcee.

We'd checked into adjoining rooms at the Ritz Carlton Hotel and gone out "on the town."

When the phone woke me, I was informed that a car would collect me at noon. I started to bath and shave when the phone rang again, to tell me that the phone in my companions adjoining room didn't answer.

"Knock on the door," I recommended, whilst continuing to shave.

I had only the vaguest recollection of how the previous night had ended. Unfortunately, I did remember one remark by my divorcee friend:

"If my husband were to find out, I'd have to kill myself."

The phone rang for the third time. It was the manager again.

"We'll have to break down the door," he declared.

I sat down on the bed, thinking that my career was at a peek—I was sure that the bad publicity would ruin my future. Little did I know what the future really had in store for me. As my life passed before me, the phone rang for the fourth time. A hung over female voice came over the phone, saying sleepily, "There is somebody at the door, darling."

With a sigh of relief I tried to sound calm, which I wasn't yet, "It's time to get up, my dear, and catch the plane."

The series of spectacular broadcasts which I had originated during the war, continued. In particular, the Daily Mail National Film Awards, had become an annual event, of which the climax was a lavish party in the ballroom of the Dorchester Hotel, where the awards were presented. The cabaret that followed was always staged as if it were an impromptu entertainment, to which some of the guests contributed.

An American singer, Hildegarde, was the latest in a sequence of stars that had appeared at that event. Hildegarde had started her career in Europe before the war and had returned to London to make a series for me. Hildegarde had a particularly obnoxious and virulent manager, Anna Sosenko, known in the business as "Anna—the Queen of I Am."

I was seated with my mother at our table in the ballroom at the Dorchester, when I was called to the phone. It was Anna from the suite upstairs at the hotel.

"Harry," she complained, "I have just learned, that last year, Gracie Fields got fifty thousand pounds for this gig and Hildy isn't coming down for less than one hundred thousand pounds—cash."

I pointed out that Gracie had donated the money to her favorite charity, an orphanage she had founded. That had no effect—so I said I would call Anna back.

As I replaced the receiver in the lobby, I noted that there appeared to be an unusual number of security guards.

I found out that upstairs, incognito, was Bing Crosby, who had just returned from a visit to the Open Gold Championship in Scotland. In the ballroom, I made contact with, perhaps, the two most attractive ladies there: An eighteen year old Jean Simmons, whom I knew well, and Lady Rothermere, our host, who reportedly was the mistress of Ian Fleming, creator of James Bond.

I took them both upstairs with me and knocked on the door of Bing Crosby's suite. Bing answered the door himself, wearing casual clothes. He invited us inside for a drink. We had a great time, but it was getting late. Finally, Bing, still in casuals, agreed to come downstairs to the elite black tie event.

The evening came to a close when Bing consented to come up on stage and sing. He was accompanied by two other guests who happened to be present—Bob Hope and Dorothy Lamour. I never called Anne Sosenko back.

The following morning, Lord Rothermere, at my suggestion, had a Georgian solid silver antique tea service delivered to Bing Crosby's suite.

I continued my activities staging events. These included the greatest ever fashion parade, with over one hundred models. I took over the Albert Hall for the Fashion Industry.

I utilized the Albert Hall again for a very different event, the first ever reunion of the RAF Bomber Command. My favorite event of all time was a Sunday night program I staged at the London Palladium, for the Water Rats, the Masonic type order, which brought together all of Britain's Music Hall, (Vaudeville) performers. The first half of the bill was composed of the world's finest "sight" acts, jugglers, bicyclists, acrobats and dancers. Custom usually allowed such acts ten to fifteen minutes on stage, but on this occasion, we limited their time to five minutes apiece. This meant that they had to concentrate all their best tricks and material in the shortest time available. The first act finale was based on the Frith print entitled "Popularity," which graced the walls at countless London pubs.

The print was of a London street scene and featured most of the great Music Hall artists of the day. On stage at the Palladium, we had the sons and daughters of these great artists from the past, singing the songs their parents made famous. The curtain rose on the second act which was being broadcast to the nation.

The set was in the traditional minstrel show pattern and seated were all the great surviving Music Hall stars, including Max Miller and the entire Crazy gang, Naughton and Gold, Nervo and Knox, Flanagan and Allen and "Monsewer" Eddie Gray. The show that followed was mainly filled with male performers until the finale, which featured the greatest of all entertainers, Gracie Fields.

The event was sponsored by the News of the World, but on Monday morning the Daily Express, perhaps the greatest competitor and rival of the News of the World, devoted the whole of its front page to a still picture of the event, with the caption: "Last night you heard it, this morning you see it."

The editor of the News of the World called me, with tears in his voice: "Harry," he said, "You've done it again." As a publicist I felt, just a little, proud.

One of the finest publicists I have ever known was, Ernie Heasman. He believed in lasting results.

"Any damn fool can get publicity by burning five pound notes in Piccadilly Circus, but good publicity is built to last—like elephant prints in cement," he used to say.

He provided a perfect example, which visitors to London can still see today, if they stroll down Piccadilly and pass St. James's Church.

During the War Years, Lord Southwood, a newspaper tycoon, used to pass this way twice a day, en route from his home in Pall Mall to his office in Fleet Street. He noticed, in passing, that the churchyard of St. James's was neglected and unkempt. Lord Southwood arranged to provide the necessary financial help to restore the churchyard.

Ernie Heasman was instructed to ensure that Lord Southwood's generosity was properly acknowledged and not forgotten. A memorial plaque, displaying Lord Southwood's name prominently as the benefactor, was added to the walls of the churchyard, facing Piccadilly for all to see. Queen Mary consented to lend her presence to the unveiling of the plaque, which was serenaded by a fanfare from the State Trumpeters. Elephant footsteps indeed.

Now back to the Music Hall, (Vaudeville).

Maria, my wife used to refer to my one liners as old radio jokes. However my jokes actually predate both radio and television.

Here are two more of my "memories":

First the British comedian who borrowed his stage name from a poster on the wall—Nosmo King (no smoking). The second, whose name I have alas forgotten was a "Quick Change Artist." He appeared twice nightly in his sketch based upon Charles Dickens novel Oliver Twist called "The Death of Nancy."

The act took place in a single set with the tabs (curtains) pulled tightly to the edges of the set. In the scene were three characters: Fagin, Bill Sykes and his girl friend Nancy. There was never more than one character on stage at the time.

For instance Fagin would be talking and then be interrupted by a knock on the door. The actor would jump out through a window and, in what seemed only a few seconds, reappear opening the door in the character of Nancy. Thus the illusion continued with at least three other quick changes.

The act had for years toured the Music Halls of the English speaking world. Then, one night, a careless stage hand forgot to close the tabs, thus exposing the tricks of the Quick Change Artist to the audience.

At the end of the act the applause far exceeded the normal ovation.

Henceforth the Quick Change Artist never had the tabs closed and toured the world with even greater success for another twenty years. Then he retired to live in Hollywood where he made a good living playing cameo roles where a British accent was an advantage. This Quick Change Artist had, without realizing it provided the inspiration for the now so popular modern television reality show. Remember this was twice nightly.

Meantime, my friendship with Gracie Fields had maintained and deepened. Recently, her second husband, Monty Banks, a successful Italian comedian and film director had tragically died, aboard a train, in Gracie's arms. She was lonely.

I remember one time, when I had met her in New York. At that time, I had sold the rights to the weekly radio shows she continued to record for me, in Australia, to Wrigley's.

I needed Gracie to record, in a New York studio, the jingle the advertising agency had designed. In her broad and unmistakable Lancashire accent, she declaimed: "Eh by goom, it's a wonderful gum."

After the recording, as she was alone, we went out on the town together. In a variety store on 42nd Street, we had our photo taken, standing behind the cut out figures of two fat ladies. I've lost the copy, which I deeply regret.

Another time in London, we met in a restaurant and I passed to her a substantial sum, in cash, her weekly living allowance. Whilst we continued our meal, Gracie counted out the cash on her lap, saying: "It isn't that I don't trust you, Harry, but if I didn't count it, you'd think I was a "moog."

One season, as Gracie had tax problems in England, we recorded the shows overseas, with audiences consisting of members of Her Majesty's Forces, stationed, at this time, in Germany. When Gracie arrived in Berlin the British Commander of the Forces in the city, had arranged a ceremonial welcome, complete with a band and a guard of honor.

I'll always remember how, when Gracie stepped out of the small chartered plane at Tempelhof Airport, she had only one hand free to acknowledge the salute. In the other Gracie carried a large Marks and Spencer shopping bag.

Before Gracie reigned as the number one star of the English Music Hall, or vaudeville, as our American cousins prefer to call it, her closest predecessor was Marie Lloyd. They shared the same kind of billing; instead of "Our Marie" it was now "Our Gracie."

I once tried to convince Gracie to portray Marie Lloyd in a film biography.

"Nay, lad," she replied, "I'm no fool, she had a better act than mine."

Years before, when Queen Victoria was in her declining years, the Old Queen, the widow of Windsor, was persuaded by her advisors, to honor the Music Hall.

She invited to Windsor all the top stars of the Halls, for a Command Performance, which later, after her death, became a yearly occasion, which continues to this day.

However, on this first occasion, there was a notable omission. Marie Lloyd was not invited.

The general opinion was that many of Marie Lloyd's best songs tended to be saucy, such as: "I always believe in having it—if you fancy it. If you fancy it, it's understood. Because a little of what you fancy—does you good."

But Marie had her revenge.

A week after the event, she topped the bill at Sir Alfred Butts Palace Theatre. She changed her billing for the occasion: "Our Marie—every night—a Command Performance."

Back to the United States.

It was around this period that I became friendly with the director, Preston Sturges. I had interviewed him at his office in the RKO Studios and we had become friends. I was waiting to see him one day, when I became conscious that I shared the waiting room with another celebrity. He appeared like a retired bank manager and it was only after talking to him that I realised he was the giant of the silent screen, Harold Lloyd. He was going to appear for Preston Sturges in a remake of the film, *Safety Last*, but it was never made.

RKO was owned at that time by the elusive Howard Hughes, whose memory has recently been revived in the film, *The Aviator*. Hughes also owned TWA and Preston suggested to me that air line flights to distant locations need no longer be a problem. But Preston himself had a problem, as his output decreased and he seemed to gently fade away after he made two expensive films for Hughes which turned out to be financial disasters. That was the end of his career.

Before that happened however, Howard Hughes made one of his rare appearances at RKO Studios. He arrived, in his chauffeur driven limousine in the middle of the night, when there was only the night watchman to greet him. After a perfunctory tour of the studios, he prepared to depart.

"Any instructions, Mr Hughes?" the night watchman anxiously enquired.

"Paint it'" said Howard Hughes as he got into his limousine and vanished into the night.

In New York, a frequent and amusing dinner companion was a young English girl, Pat Marlow. I'd first met Pat in London, when I was introduced to her by her boy friend, Ernie Ponticella, the accompanist to the popular singer, Donald Peers, who was under contract to me. She was then a teenager, animated and quite attractive. I remember that, when we met she was wearing an angora sweater without a brassiere, not at all usual in those days.

I heard rumors that Pat had been involved with many members of the Music Hall professions and, finally, the band leader and impresario, Jack Hylton. Jack had made Pat the mistress of ceremonies of a touring discovery show. Ben Warris, the witty and rather cruel half of the variety act, Jewel and Warris, had, again according to rumors, sent Pat a congratulatory telegram for her opening night, signed by everybody with whom she had slept during the previous year.

In 1954, mother and I attended the Royal Command Performance Variety Show. It was held that year at the Victoria Palace, which was owned by Jack Hylton. Pat sat in his box which was immediately opposite the Royal Box.

Jack Hylton was married at that time and Pat Marlow was discretely hidden by the curtains of the box, except for her hands, which were clearly visible.

For those who knew Pat well, like me, we were very aware of her presence.

The show was compèred by Tommy Trinder and the finale featured the entire cast of *Annie Get Your Gun* that was currently playing in London.

Ethel Merman flew in especially from New York to appear in *There is no Business like Show Business*. At that time I had a Jaguar and a driver named Dan. After the performance ended mother and I were looking for our car. When we finally found it, Dan was fast asleep in the back seat.

He woke startled and blurted out: "I've warmed the seat for you, ma'am."

When I met Pat again in New York, she was living in an apartment provided for her by Jack Hylton. Her circle of acquaintances had grown extensively, including Cantinflas, the Mexican comedian, who starred in Michael Todd's *Around the World in Eighty Days*.

Pat had been staying with Jack Warner, of Warner Brothers, at his house in Beverly Hills on Angelino Drive. They had had a row and Pat had moved into the Beverly Hilton Hotel. In an effort to apologize for his rudeness,

Jack Warner offered to buy her lunch before she left for New York. As the meal neared its end and Pat was about to depart, Jack asked her how she had passed the morning.

"Shopping," she responded.

Jack asked her what she bought, emphasizing that whatever it is should, of course, be charged to her room, for which he was paying the bill.

"Just a coat," was her reply.

"What color?" he enquired.

"White," was the answer as she got up to leave, before delivering her exit line: "Mink."

Pat had, in fact, charged a US$ 20,000 mink coat to her room. Pat was a very entertaining lady and I do mean conversationally speaking.

Just one week after Marilyn Monroe's death, I was sad to hear that Pat Marlow had been found dead in the London apartment she occupied, in the mews off Park Lane, opposite the Dorchester Hotel. There was very little news coverage and I don't remember reading any reports of an inquest. Years later, an investigative journalist, who had found out that I had known Pat, came to interview me. From him, I first learned that Pat was pregnant when she died and, reputedly, the father was a prominent member of the Royal family.

I used Pat's name and her life as an inspiration for a screenplay I have written and hope to produce, entitled *Command Performance*.

I offered the leading role to Monica Lewinsky, who was amused but declined, proclaiming that she didn't want to be an actress.

It's a great part but difficult to cast. I'm still looking for "Pat Marlow."

By this time I had already become a regular visitor to Los Angeles, where so many of the British actresses I had first known and met during the war, had now become Hollywood stars. These include Jean Simmons and Deborah Kerr.

Deborah, who I had known from the start of her career, had been hired by MGM, as a threat to Greer Garson. In those days, Howard Dietz, their brilliant Head of Publicity, had created the annual slogan, not only featured on the billboards, but a compulsory postscript to any letter written by an MGM executive, worldwide.

With the advent Deborah, the annual slogan had become: "Deborah Kerr – Rhymes with Star."

On one occasion, the doorman at the Mocambo, a popular night spot on Sunset Boulevard, announced to her, when a limo arrived to take her home: "Your Cur, Miss Car."

Next year, the slogan became: "I Love Lilli," promoting the title role of a popular MGM film at the time. I remember, when in Manila, en route to Tokyo, hearing the MGM branch manager dictating a letter to a distributor on one of the islands, who had become delinquent in his remittances.

In brutal terms he was advised that, not only, would he receive no more MGM films, but the boycott would extend to all Hollywood product, until he, and his family were brought to their knees and starving.

The branch manager closed his letter with the obligatory: "P.S. I Love Lilli."

But back to happier memories of Sunset Boulevard.

I recall one evening at Ciro's, when Lucille Ball was introduced by Dezi Arnaz, whose orchestra provided the music at Ciro's, in a comedy routine, which was to provide the inspiration for her long running television series *I Love Lucy*.

The audience included Errol Flynn, accompanied by a young Marilyn Monroe, who disappeared beneath the table cloth, leaving Errol Flynn with a big smile on his face.

In Hollywood, both then and now, breakfast is dominated by a sight of the morning "trades." First comes the New York based *Variety*, followed by its Los Angeles based rival the *Hollywood Reporter*. *Variety* prides itself on the integrity of its critics, where often the products of some of its biggest advertisers are the subject of scathing reviews.

Some claim that the *Hollywood Reporter* offers the certainty of receiving favorable reviews from its critics, via the office of the advertising manager.

Variety has its own inimitable language. Beginning with the famous headline on the day that New York's Stock Market collapsed, heralding the Great Depression: "Wall Street Lays An Egg."

The tradition continues. When Laurence Olivier's classic film version of Shakespeare's *Henry V* first hit the screen, *Variety* christened it "Hank Cinq."

On another occasion Laurence Olivier and Vivien Leigh graced Broadway with their performances in Shakespeare's *Anthony and Cleopatra* and Bernard Shaw's *Ceasar and Cleopatra*, *Variety* matched the theatergoers frequent demand for "two on the aisle" with the description of the event as "two on the Nile."

Chapter Five
King of Radio,
But for How Long?

B y the 1950's our radio business was very successful. We had a series scheduled, in prime time, on four American Networks. In the U.K. we dominated the market on Radio Luxembourg and had, by selling shows to the BBC, cracked open their monopoly.

Our associate Towers of London companies in Australia, South Africa and Canada, were all achieving healthy sales. When I started to go regularly to the US, I quickly learned about the night life of New York

I soon acquired a lady friend, who was in the chorus line at the Copacabana, a very famous night club near the Plaza Hotel. The rule at the Copacabana was that no girl could be any taller than 5'2" because the ceiling of the stage at the Copa was only 6 feet.

My lady friend would meet me after her show in the lounge at the Plaza hotel and then we would walk back to my apartment on West 58thStreet and have a wonderful time.

I had another girl friend at that time, who worked in the Latin Quarter run by Lou Walters the father of the famous and enduringly beautiful Barbara Walters; (there's a 'Lou Walters Way' in N.Y. now.)

The girl I knew from the Latin Quarter was an exceptionally beautiful, Japanese show girl. I often used to take her out on the town after her show. This was just after the end of the war and there were very few new Japanese girls arriving in New York. She had managed to get into the United States by being the girl friend of the Head of the International Wool Secretariat.

There was only one good Japanese Restaurant in New York City at the time, which also served Japanese beer.

My mother was a very frequent visitor to New York, in those days. I remember her insisting that my beautiful Japanese girl friend take off her kimono and dress again, so my Mother could see exactly how kimonos were actually put on. Although I was quite used to seeing my friend undressed, mother's request was really rather embarrassing

This is another little story about my mother in New York. When I took her to a night club on central park, called the Penthouse, (it no longer exists), the young lady was very impressed with meeting my mother and said, "I am so proud to meet you. I have heard so much about you from your son. I must tell you that you remind me very much of a well known English stage and screen actress." Mother, hoping the girl was going to mention someone like Greer Garson, said "Oh really, my dear, who did you have in mind"? My sweet, little friend said, "Hermione Gingold."

End of story; end of friendship.

I had acquired a publicity agent by the name of Chris Cross. He did a fine job for me. I got coverage in the *New Yorker* magazine and all the trade papers. In February of 1952 I was featured in *Time Magazine* and, on my 32nd birthday, I was profiled in the *New York Times*.*

Despite everything looking rosy, I was well aware that our dependency on radio meant that our days were numbered. I saw the future of radio as, basically, a source of music and news. For my swan song in radio, we produced and sold a package of 260 new shows, with the title *The World's Greatest Mysteries* with Basil Rathbone as the host.

Looming ahead was 1955, which would be a significant year in my life.

The British Government had finally decided to permit commercial television in the United Kingdom. The 'Independent Television Authority' had been created to grant licenses to aspiring Program Contractors and to provide the broadcasting facilities. Norman Collins, who had headed the BBC Television services, was clearly a potential candidate.

Together with the electronics firm of Pye of Cambridge and its forceful CEO, C.O. Stanley, they had launched a new technical facility, High Definition Films, which was little more than a high quality telecine.

They had taken over Highbury Studios and I became their tenant. I immediately started production of a half hour drama anthology series, later released in the US under the title *Lilli Palmer Presents.*

I also produced yet another pilot, for a series based on *The Annals of the British institute for Psychic Research.*

The first episode was inspired by the theory that Jack the Ripper was really a member of the British Royal Family. Broderick Crawford was the host and narrator. We never made the series, but the idea was utilized, recently, as the subject for a feature film *From Hell* with Johnny Depp as Inspector Frederick Abberline.

I also made a pilot film for *The Adventures of the Scarlet Pimpernel* featuring the same star as the radio series, Marius Goring. During this busy period of my life, I was also involved in the production of a film entitled *The Anatomist* based on the true story of Burke and Hare, starring Alistair Sim.

I conceived a series of spectacular revues and hired a successful television director, Henry Caldwell, to direct the first of them in Paris.

---

* http://www.time.com/time/magazine/article/0,9171,822157,00.html
http://select.nytimes.com/gst/abstract.html?res=F70710FD3A5B117A93CBA8178BD95F468585F9

KING OF RADIO, BUT FOR HOW LONG?

We took over the Moulin Rouge for a week and I made a deal with Ed Sullivan to also originate part of his highly popular weekly series on CBS. This was before transatlantic television was a technical possibility, but we planned to film and edit the segment and rush it to New York to air the same week.

I had brought my mother with me to Paris, where she loved to go shopping. We occupied a suite at the George V. At dinner that evening, I remembered that the editor had given me

the air-waybill for the consignment to New York. I excused my self and told mother that I had to make a phone call.

On the phone I learned, to my horror that the package was on a flight due to arrive on Monday morning. In my pocket, burning a hole, was a cheque for $100,000, given to me by Ed Sullivan's manager before he left.

The show was scheduled to air on Sunday. I jumped into a cab and headed to Orly airport. I managed to locate the package and was lucky enough to find a captain of a delayed flight, who agreed to carry the package and deliver the film in New York on Saturday.

It was long past midnight, when I returned to my mother in the George V. hotel. My mother was used to me appearing and disappearing at a moment's notice, so I didn't need to explain, I would have been too tired in any case.

Chapter Six

Success, and then Disaster

The Independent Television Authority (ITA) was ready to listen to applications for a license. Commercial Television was to make its debut in the UK in September of 1955. Associated Newspapers, who owned the Daily Mail, had decided to go into business with Re-diffusion, where I had already been a steady provider of radio programs.

As I was also under contract as a consultant to the Daily Mail, it looked as though I had another possible television home. However, Mike Nidorf, a very experienced American talent agent, who I knew well, had another idea. Mike had brought together his fellow agents, Lew and Leslie Grade, as well as the Moss Empire Theatre Group and other powerful show business forces, to form a new company.

I was invited to join the board and become a major stockholder of the new company, which was, ultimately, to become Associated Television, ATV and its production associate ITC. Financial interests in the city convinced the Norman Collins Group to merge with ATV. At the initial meeting with ITA, I was the spokesperson for the enlarged group.

Sir Robert Fraser, CEO of the newly formed ITA, asked Prince Littler, chairman of Moss Empires, whether he might, unofficially, turn to me as a consultant. Prince agreed and the following day, I met privately with Sir Robert Fraser.

Sir Robert told me then of his plan to use the example of the newspaper industry to divide his license on a regional basis, with different contractors for the weekday and weekend concessions. I pointed out to Robert that with initially only one channel for each region, the result would be that he was simply appointing the shareholders, in what would inevitably become, a network monopoly. This is exactly what has happened recently.

In the final disposition of licenses, ATV was granted the license for the weekend programming in London and the complete week for the Midlands. I became the Program Director for ATV and faced the challenge to provide, in a matter of months, a brand new television service, which had hitherto been a monopoly of the BBC.

I set to work immediately, asking selected personnel from the BBC to join our new venture. The BBC was the only source for experienced television technicians. This was the busiest and most exhilarating period of my life and I thoroughly enjoyed the challenge.

In New York, for a change, I was now the buyer and not the seller. The BBC, as the only British customer, had neglected to tie up the main program sources in the US. Thus, we, the new boys in town, could lay our hands on the cream of the syndicated product and secure the television debut in the UK of such, soon to be familiar titles as *I Love Lucy*, *Liberace*, and *Dragnet*.

Variety, the number one entertainment trade paper, ran a full page, devoted to my many activities, which they headlined: "Up and Up with Towers."

Around this time Lew Wasserman—head of MCA (Music Corporation of America) arrived in London.

Lew Grade, my fellow director in ATV rushed into the modest office we shared in Regent Street, "Lew Wasserman is in London, at Claridges Hotel. He wants us to go and see him."

"Lew" I replied "We are buying not selling—Wasserman comes to see us."

And so he did.

I explained to Lew Wasserman that we had already agreed with the other program contractors that we would limit the price we paid for American production to two thousand Pounds per half hour.

"So?" replied Lew Wasserman. "It's another monopoly, just like the BBC.

No point then, in discussing the price—just tell me which of our series do you want to buy?"

Years afterwards, when I met again with Lew Wasserman, he raised his hat to me. I felt a little proud at that moment. Lew Wasserman's life was immortalized in the TV documentary *The Last Mogul*.

Our main asset, in securing the maximum audience of viewers, was our unrivalled position to provide the very best in British performers.

Val Parnell's *Sunday Night at the London Palladium* was our star attraction. It was to be the mainstay of the new commercial network for years to come.

I was able to secure a place for my entire product and, in particular, the Towers of London drama output on High Definition from Highbury Studios.

I founded yet another company, with Richard Meyer and Maurice Goodman, to make the commercials. We converted an old cinema in Barnes and turned it into another studio. One of our employees was Ridley Scott, who has since become a very famous film director.

Through a mutual friend, Dale Gordon, Roy Rogers' wife, we gained an introduction to the Reverend Billy Graham, then visiting London on one of his spiritual crusades. Lew Grade and I visited the Reverend at a Knightsbridge hotel and got him interested in the idea of filming a series of thirteen sermons, provided he, very astutely, retained the copyright in the negative for his foundation. As we walked down the corridor, after leaving the suite, Billy called out after us: "Hey, Lew, you'll get your commission in Heaven."

When we were filming the sermons with Billy, he obviously knew the tradition, that on the last day of shooting, the star gives a present to the crew.

He gave each one a big, brown envelope containing a presentation copy of the Holy Bible. Only those crew members who actually opened the bible discovered that, lodged inside the Holy Book, was another, smaller envelope, containing a five pound note.

As the opening date for the London transmitter grew nearer, so did the fever of preparation. On opening night, my mother and I dined, with my fellow directors, at the old Embassy Club in Bond Street. Everybody congratulated me on the achievement. The next few weeks saw the pioneering operation settling down and continue to grow.

An old friend, Orson Welles, was in town. He had just played the preacher in John Huston's *Moby Dick*, starring Gregory Peck and was now staging his own version of Herman Melville's classic at the Duke of York's Theatre, with himself as Captain Ahab and Joan Plowright as the Cabin Boy.

Joan was ultimately to become the last wife of Lord Laurence Olivier.

After seeing the imaginative theatre version, in which the setting was an empty stage, where a group of traveling players extemporized the tale, I went backstage to congratulate Orson.

I was accompanied by a very experienced film technician, David MacDonald, who had directed *Desert Victory* and who was working for me at the time on a television series. Orson proposed to me that we should rent a theatre and go into immediate production of a film of his stage version, which would be ready for release well ahead of the Gregory Peck film.

MacDonald, in a whisper, warned me that to endeavor to translate the stage production into a film could be a disaster.

"You're a coward, Harry Towers," proclaimed Orson after I voiced my reservations.

Orson found another financial backer, rented a theatre and started shooting the movie version. When he viewed the rushes after three weeks of filming, he left and never showed up for the fourth week and the project was abandoned.

Many years later, I tried to locate this footage as well as other films Orson never completed, including; *Don Quixote* with Akim Tamiroff as Sancho Panza. (After Orson's death in 1985, Jesus Franco finally finished this project in 1992.)

There were a few of such uncompleted films.

I planned to assemble the footage and present a selection of the best scenes, with Orson being interviewed by Wolf Mankowitz, and also provide the commentary, entitled *They Never Let Me Finish It*.

The project never materialized during Orson's life time. I believe, the reason was that ultimately Orson realized, deep in his own heart that "they" were, in fact himself."

In 1955, I spent Christmas and the New Year on a trip to Australia, on behalf of Associated Newspapers.

The Australian government was about to grant licenses in the major cities for commercial TV stations and my friends at the Daily Mail wanted a piece of the action. I spent two weeks, together with my good friend Stuart Maclean and such legendary newspaper proprietors as Frank Packer and Sir Keith Murdoch. The then rumors, have in the meantime, been verified. Stuart Maclean, in addition to his work in the newspaper world, also had close ties with British Intelligence.

The events, some years ahead, were to provide the missing link. Whilst many years have passed, I must still stay silent on some of the details.

When I returned to London, after the holidays, I found out that I was in big trouble.

My fellow directors at ATV had gotten together, behind my back, and decided to diminish my responsibilities. On my highway to success, I had ridden too hard and had antagonized many of my colleagues and peers. To add to my trouble, a minor deal to which I was a party indicated a potential conflict of interest. On top of that, I had failed to control the finances of the many operations in which I was involved and they were in a precarious position. In short, I was in a heck of a mess and only had myself to blame.

I resigned from the board and sold my shares. I was, incidentally, the largest stockholder in ATV.

With a heavy heart, I had to put Production Services, my holding company, into liquidation. The party was over. I went back to New York determined to rebuild my life.

I had continued to maintain my apartment at the Hotel Meurice on W.58th Street. As I was so frequently elsewhere, I agreed, on occasions, to let some of my friends use it. Among these friends was a young lady called Elena Da Vinci who, ultimately, became the wife of a prominent Los Angeles dental surgeon. When I knew Elena, she was single and had a small, but elegant home on Beverly Canyon, Beverly Hills.

I came to an arrangement with Elena that, when I was in L.A. and she was out of town, I could use her house and, if I was not in N.Y., she could have access to my apartment there.

The Hotel Meurice had a very obtrusive night manager, who, late one night, when I was out of town, became aware of an unknown visitor, who refused to leave the lobby.

Elena called me and, ultimately, her guest, none other than then Senator John F. Kennedy, had to come to the lobby himself to explain, that the man was a detective and his personal body guard. My continuing association with JFK did not go unnoticed by J. Edgar Hoover which would turn out to be a truly tragic episode in my life.

I did not always move in such exalted circles, but my life in New York and London continued. Luckily, my friends at the Ziv Company entrusted me with producing the first Anglo-American syndicated international Television Series, *Martin Kane* starring, William Gargan. We went into production at the Associated British Studios, at the, heretofore unheard of rate, of two programs a week.

After twenty weeks of crazy and hectic activity, we completed the initial series of thirty nine programs, on budget and on schedule. My relationship with Bill Gargan had deteriorated to such an extent that, when on the last day of shooting, he went on strike. I sent a message to his dressing room that, I wanted him back on the set "dead or alive" and he could guess in which condition I would prefer him.

In my car, on the way back into town and the Dorchester Hotel, where Bill was staying, he was strangely silent. Finally, he asked me if I had really wished him dead.

Still rather irritated with him, I replied, "No, just sick enough so we could collect the insurance without having to endure your presence."

Bill never spoke to me again.

That night we had a "wrap" party at which I took out on the town a number of those comrades who had helped make my return to television a success. They included the Art Director, Frank White, the director, Bob Lynn and the Production Manager, John Comfort, I took them all to Murray's Cabaret Club and we had a great time together.

As *Martin Kane* had been a financial success I was able to buy my mother a country cottage near Telscombe. It was the first country home she had ever owned. In the past, the property where she lived and I spent the weekend had always been rented.

I sometimes wonder what has happened to my comrades. Some may still be alive. If so, I wish them well. I remember them as true friends. If they are still alive, I hope they remember me.

During the making of *Martin Kane*, we filmed the pilot for another series, *DIAL 999* that soon went into production. I utilized my knowledge of London's "20,000 streets beneath the sky" that I learnt as a young teenager from R.G.Jones of Morden, to help me find the locations.

In addition, I was making other series, *Tales from Dickens* with Fredric March as the host and an ambitious musical series with many famous guests called: *Mantovani*.

It was during this period, that my then N.Y. attorney, Warren Troob, who was going to be of invaluable assistance to me, in times to come, introduced me to Alan Freed, the disk jockey on WINS, who originated the words: "Rock and Roll" and was the first disk jockey to play Rock and Roll, against the Station Manager's judgment. He was a great success.

I became friends with Freed and arranged to record his commentary and send it together with the records to Radio Luxemburg, where it was broadcast regularly.

When TV caught up with Alan Freed, he was hired by one of the Networks, to do a weekly TV Show. The mixture of African American and white artists together created a scandal and Alan was fired.

Thereafter, Alan's life was a very sad one. He could no longer work in N.Y., developed a number of ailments, but really died of a broken heart, six years later. Many of us miss him. He was a pioneer—misunderstood—ahead of his time.

I was still commuting between London and New York when the original production of *My Fair Lady* opened on Broadway. The seats were the hottest tickets in town. Two of my friends headed the cast. Stanley Holloway and Julie Andrews, who first came to the States in *The Boy Friend*.

It was Stanley who told me one of the best theatre stories I have ever heard. Every performance of *My Fair Lady* was a complete sellout. However, during the first week, at a Saturday matinee, one of the seats in the stalls was noticeably empty. The house manager and the company publicist, sensing a story went, during the interval to talk to the little senior lady, who occupied the adjoining isle seat.

She explained that it was her husband who, hearing of the production, was lucky enough to get two stalls, to celebrate their fortieth wedding anniversary.

After she told them that her husband had died last week, the manager could not help but ask her, if she could not have brought a friend or relative? "Not really," she replied. "It's the funeral this afternoon."

Around this time, after the Cannes Film Festival, I found myself in the same departure lounge with Lew Grade at Nice airport. Despite my differences with my fellow directors at ATV, I had always remained friends with Lew. We discussed the continuing policy of the major studios in Hollywood to boycott the ever-growing power of the US television networks. I suggested to Lew, that ATV might break that ban by favoring a single American network with a deal. Lew took my advice and made a fortune for ATV and himself.

That same year I wrote and produced the pilot film for a syndicated television series entitles: *King of Diamonds*, starring Broderick Crawford shot partially in an L.A. Studio with the balance of the filming on location in Brussels and Antwerp.

The pilot was ultimately successful and the series produced. Unfortunately by that time the fates had intervened and I was not available to produce the remaining episodes.

By 1959, I was back in full independent production, but I still needed a network sale in the US. I had produced a One Hour Pilot for a series entitled *Crime Club*.

The initial episode was a dramatization of a Cornell Woolrich story *You'll Never See Me Again* starring Ben Gazarra with Ted Post directing. NBC had seen the pilot and really liked it. I sold the initial thirteen films to the Kraft Company, as the summer replacement for the Perry Como show.

I intended to include, in the first thirteen shows, the maximum number of pilot films, for other potential series. I had already secured, from the writer, Leslie Charteris, the rights for *The Saint*.

By now, I had given up my lease on my living quarters at the Meurice Hotel and had moved into an apartment on West 56th Street. It was an evening in January 1961. I was working in my office at the apartment, when fate dealt me another blow. I had developed a friendship with an attractive, eighteen year old model, Mariella Novotny, and I had invited her to come to New York with me.

During the December holiday season, I went back to London to be with my mother. Mariella asked if she could stay on at my N.Y. apartment, whilst I was abroad. I agreed. I returned to New York after the holidays. Mariella and I had a serious disagreement and she moved out.

On that fateful evening, I mentioned earlier, Mariella called me and asked if she could meet somebody at my place. I was very busy, but I agreed anyway. Big mistake!

I was sitting at my typewriter, working away, when the door to the office burst open. Mariella, stark naked, screamed that she had been arrested.

When I talked to the detective from the vice squad, who was making the arrest, I naturally told him, that the lease of the apartment was in my name. As we all left the apartment together, Mariella was greeted by a man I had never met. I learned later that it was her husband, Hod Dibben, a somewhat shady art dealer, whom Mariella was living with at Essex House on Central Park South. I assume that he followed her to New York, when he realized that she would be staying there. Quite overwhelmed and confused, I thought it best to call my attorney before making any kind of statements.

Mariella was accusing me of importing her into the US for immoral purposes, as well as that I was living off her earnings as a high class call girl. In reality, she used those earnings to keep her husband in the money.

My arrest made the headlines in New York. It was even worse in London, where my name was much better known. It was when I was first charged at the Precinct Station and I was asked to remove my belt and braces to avoid any opportunity of a suicide attempt and led to a cell for the few remaining hours of the night that I began to fully realize the desperate situation I was in.

During the following days when I remained in confinement, did I ever consider suicide? Of course I did, but I dismissed the thought immediately. I knew instinctively that I had too much to live for.

Now, looking back in time, little did I know that the forthcoming period I was to spend behind the Iron Curtain, would have a profound effect on my entire future, which I felt was at stake. To misquote Charles Dickens, from the *Tale of Two Cities*, for reasons of deception and not the truth, this was to be "the only way"—for a condemned man the rescuer would have to face the guillotine.

It is far too early in this biography, to raise the question of my epitaph, but raise it I will.

I quote, again pessimistically the Victorian saying: "It wasn't the cough that carried him off, it was the coffin they carried him off in."

Or, more optimistically to quote the reasoning of an old man: "They don't write songs like they used to anymore."

The response from a still older man: "They never did."

As I will relate later, had this terrible incident not occurred, I would probably never have met my wonderful wife Maria.

My bail was set at $100,000, which was an amount I could not raise. Scared out my mind, in my prison cell, in the Tombs, the Manhattan House of Detention, which was full of addicts and other detainees, screaming, crying out and shouting, banging and kicking the bars—a veritable Hell on Earth, I felt like this was the end of my life—and I wished it were.

I knew I was not guilty of anything I was being accused of. Despite feeling desperately upset and anxious, I sat down to write, in long hand, a story of my life. Within a week, my London agent, David Higham, had sold my story to the News of the World for fifty thousand pounds.

Another week later, I was freed, my bail reduced, but with a further Federal charge against me. I felt so desperate, with my career in ruins.

My name was taken off all the shows I had on the air in the US.

My mother joined me from London and I started to prepare my defense

I quickly found, after investigation, that although I was completely innocent of any of the charges, there was enough circumstantial evidence, for the case to go to trial. I also realized that my limited resources would soon be exhausted by all the lawyer fees etc. I saw myself be left penniless and unable to combat the effect that the trial, irrespective of the outcome, would have upon my future.

I could not go through with it. I knew I was innocent—how could I prove it? I had to get away, get some distance; I couldn't even think straight. I decided that the only way was to leave the US. I drove across the border to Canada and took a plane to Europe.

I gave a final interview to the News of the World in Copenhagen and caught the afternoon flight to Moscow. A new adventure had begun!

You will appreciate that this was a time of destiny, not just for me, but for the entire western world.

The Cold War was at its height, but at the same time, the relationship, between the Soviet Union and China, had become extremely frosty.

I had wanted to travel, via the Trans Siberian railway, from Moscow to Peking and write about my experiences. The official friends I had made in Russia did their best to discourage me, from even attempting, to take that trip.

Many years later, I used this idea as the inspiration for the screenplay I wrote *Bullet to Beijing* and then produced the movie, in conjunction with Showtime. When I visited the Chinese Embassy, I saw that the building was surrounded by police. I found myself enveloped I an atmosphere of suspicion.

I learned later, that these 'official friends', were convinced that my experiences in New York had all been a gigantic ruse, to give the impression to the Russian authorities that I was a fugitive from the West, and could therefore be trusted. I had to somehow win their confidence.

As a boy, I had given up the profession, but now I found myself acting for my life. In Moscow, in order to provide a cover story, I joined a group of tourists on a visit to Stalingrad, followed by a journey by river boat on the Volga/Don Canal to Rostov on Don.

It was there that the Moscow correspondent for the Daily Mail, Victor Louis, who also moonlighted as an officer in the KGB, found me and broke the story to the Daily Mail. Many years later I introduced Victor Louis as a character in the film *Bullet to Beijing*.

The world press, in particular the British and American Media, picked up the story from the Daily Mail and accused me of being an identified Soviet agent. I was quite the opposite of that, but had to stay silent. I had no alternative.

From Rostov on Don, I went to Succi on the Black Sea and then continued back to Kiev and Leningrad, which thirty years later reverted to its original name—St. Petersburg.

I decided that I would extend my tour of Eastern Europe, where I was advised I could still continue to render useful service.

I left for Moscow. When I wanted to catch an evening plane to Prague, I found that it would not be leaving before the following morning.

As Moscow had no airport hotel, I found myself sitting, all alone, as the only customer in the airport restaurant, which was about to close. I invited the waitress and the chef to join me for a night cap. After our second bottle of vodka, my new friends offered to provide me with some accommodation for the night.

They took me to the airport manager's office, and using table cloth, made a bed for me on the couch. Next morning I was even served coffee, which I can say I needed badly. Catching the morning plane, I could not help but compare the warm hospitality I had received there, with the welcome I would have received in London or New York.

After spending some weeks in Prague, I caught the midnight train to Budapest, which sounds as romantic as it felt. But romance had little to do with my journey. Whilst I was in Hungary, the Berlin Wall was erected overnight. Not my fault.

I had added new contacts and friends, from Prague and Budapest, to my ever expanding list.

The advance information I got from them, about the current and future intentions and plans, all had value, as I later learned. In Hungary, I visited Lake Balaton and continued to enjoy evenings in the theatre, as I had done in Russia and Prague. I developed a strong taste for opera, which was really the only stage attraction I could truly understand.

Still the newspapers and magazines in Britain and the US kept up their wild barrage of insults and attacks against me. The *New York Times* accused me of being a Colonel in the KGB. The *London Daily Telegraph* regaled its readers with tales of a life of luxury I was supposedly enjoying behind the Iron Curtain.

Whilst my silence continued I thought a lot about the future, including my own. I had no illusions. The terrible publicity I had received, both from the initial accusations, as well as my subsequent decision to leave the US, seemed to make any return to television virtually impossible. I needed a really original project that could be successful in any language and may help me to overcome the resistance I feared.

Suddenly, I had the idea.

A new series about a profession that is truly international. Whatever city one finds oneself in, one can always find a taxi. So what about a series about taxi drivers and how, despite a multitude of difficulties and dangers they somehow survived, no matter where. I had the inspiration of setting the initial episode in Berlin, where our driver finds himself marooned in East Berlin. We tell the story of his ultimate escape across the Wall.

I wrote the script and now needed financing.

I returned to London, incognito, and sought the help of an old friend, Howard Thomas, later the head of Thames Television.

Howard agreed to buy the *Taxi* series.

Back in West Berlin, I went to work. I brought a tiny crew from London, headed by the camera man, Nicholas Roeg. We shot and completed the film in record time. We then shot one story line in Prague and another one in Budapest and so on. Also, at this time, I produced a pilot film for a TV series, called *High Adventure*. I shot the film in the high Tatras Mountains on the border of Czechoslovakia and Poland.

I sold the pilot, never made the series, but used the same title, for a feature film, which I made in Bulgaria, many years later. The months had passed by and it was now two years since my debacle in New York. I was thinking of becoming a film producer.

I knew from experience, that a reputation of morality was definitively not an essential condition for this occupation.

Chapter Seven
I am a Film Producer

I had become aware that Edgar Wallace was still a magic name in the German cinema. Nobody remembered the Edgar Wallace classic *Sanders of the River*. This adventure-based tale, unlike Wallace's London based crime novels, was set in Africa. The rights were owned by London Films, heir to the Korda Estate, now controlled by a very dear old friend, Robert Clark. Robert made the rights available and I was able to make a deal with the major German Distributor, Constantin Film.

I signed the English star, Richard Todd, for the lead and left for Africa to raise the rest of the money. I could never have made this film without Robert Clark's help and guidance. Toward the end of Bob's life, I had the privilege of inviting him to lunch in London, together with a mutual friend.

When we asked Bob why, despite his unique contribution to the British Film Industry, he had received no official recognition, he replied as the Scot he was, "Cash for Honors— they never put it in writing"

In 1963, I started filming in St Lucia, in Natal, and five weeks later the materials went to the cutting room and, once again, the project came in on schedule and on budget. When the film opened in Germany, it was a smash hit. I was filled with gratitude. Constantin wanted to make a sequel.

I was available, very available.

By Christmas, I was back in South Africa, shooting *Table Bay* in Cape Town, starring Lex Barker, famous for his role as Tarzan and now extremely popular in Germany as Old Shatterhand, based on the Winnetou novels by the German writer Karl May. I also remembered some unused footage we had from *Taxi* that I could easily expand into a feature film. The film was called *City of Fear*.

For the star of this black and white movie, I had signed Terry Moore, who was secretly Mrs. Howard Hughes. Needing to shoot some additional footage in Austria, I went to Vienna to complete the casting. In the famous café at the Hotel Sacher, I met a young actress, Helga Maria Grohman, who was to change my life.

Maria was a really beautiful, angelic looking, eighteen year old Viennese actress, with the most memorable eyes. Since age four, Maria had been working on stage in the world famous Wiener Burgtheater and was praised as a Wunderkind.

As I later learned, Maria's father was an aristocrat persecuted by the Nazis her mother had also died and she now lived, rather unhappily, with her very ill step-mother. We met again in Munich for her screen test. Maria got the part and we got to know each other better during the filming of the movie in Salzburg.

One evening, when I had an argument with the director, I felt Maria's delicate, reassuring and supportive hand on my arm—I knew I had found a very special friend.

I persuaded her to change her name, for international movie audiences, to Maria Rohm. Had I finally found the right girl? Was I falling in love? I did not know. In the next ten years, Maria was to appear in many of the films I continued to produced, in many different countries.

We were destined to travel the world together and thus, my world became a warmer and better place in which to live. I was then, still, in my early days as a film producer and, at this stage thought about making movies in interesting and photogenic places. I wanted to bring the world to the audience.

First, I continued to explore the breathtaking country of South Africa, by making *Coast of Skeletons* again with Richard Todd, in Durban and Namibia.

I also shot *Mozambique* there, starring Hildegard Neff and Steve Cochran.

Flipper had just been a big success. Looking out over the ocean every day, I thought of making *Sandy the Seal*. Turned out not to be my best idea.

I hired three seals. They must have been on vacation from their circus performances for quite some time. They were very unruly, to put it mildly. On the first day, during filming, one of the seals took off into the Indian Ocean, heading for Australia. On the second day, one of the two remaining seals, decided to bite the hand of the young South African boy, who was playing the leading role. From then on the boy was too frightened to even touch the seal.

I managed to get a stuffed baby seal, which we, henceforth, used for everything, including the cast photo, for publicity purposes, in which the seal occupied the central position.

My American partner and long time friend, Oliver Unger, remarked: "That animal looks stuffed."

I assured him that this was not only true about the seal.

My next project *Twenty Four Hours to Kill* took me to Beirut in the Lebanon. It was an adventure story, where an aircraft has to make a forced landing and what ensued during the twenty four hour stopover.

Lex Barker played the pilot, Mickey Rooney the Steward and Walter Slezak the boss of the smugglers. As part of our financing, I had an American Letter of Credit, which I discounted with a small local bank in Beirut. The owner of the bank elected to only advance us money when he was in the right mood.

The bill at the Phoenicia Hotel, where the cast and crew were staying, had grown alarmingly high. I discretely left for London, where I met with the Completion Guarantors and its very British and forceful proprietor, Colonel Davis.

"I thought so," he declared, "an American letter of credit and a foreign bank.

Luckily, a friendly banker, Singer and Friedlander came to our aid and we successfully continued production.

We filmed the finale, for three days, in the Casino Liban. During this time, Mickey Rooney gambled and lost not only all his cash, but also his passport and his ticket home.

His ticket, we replaced.

One day, Nadia Gamel, a famous belly dancer, who had been the favorite of King Farouk of Egypt, stormed into the production office, asking where I could be found, because she had a complaint which later turned out to be just a minor misunderstanding. When asked why she wanted to see me, her response was memorable, "Because I want to kill him but very, very slowly."

Another member of the cast was the very attractive and well developed, French actress, France Anglade. The crew referred to her obvious assets as "busty substances" and it was rumored that one of the prop men was always standing by, on set, with a couple of warm spoons, just in case anything should, unexpectedly, "pop out."

Which reminds me of a popular British starlet, who I used to know, Zena Marshall. She once attended the Argentinean Film Festival at a seaside resort in Buenos Aires, when there was a knock at her bedroom door.

A charming, young Argentinean man introduced himself, "My name is Carlos and I am your escort. Please use me."

Zena was the wife of the bandleader Paul Adams. Once, when in New York, we stood, having drinks together at the rooftop bar of a skyscraper hotel, overlooking the East River. Every time Zena finished her drink, she tossed the empty glass over the parapet, so that it landed on the street below.

I still have visions of potentially blind New Yorkers cursing, to this day, the person who thoughtlessly robbed them of their sight. Think of that, Miss Marshall, wherever you are.

My active present life was still occasionally interrupted by unpleasant reminders of my recent, very difficult past. One day, after boarding the plane from London to Munich, an inexperienced and over zealous officer from MI5, had recognized my name and intercepted the flight before takeoff. Under police escort, I had to leave the aircraft in the middle of the runway. I got my luggage, which contained the cutting copy of my last film. A phone call from the MI5 officer to his superiors quickly sorted the matter out.

I received a profuse apology and the MI5 officer, personally, carried my heavy bags back to the check-in counter; not an episode for the weak at heart. From then on, I always received a happy and welcoming smile from the MI5 officer on duty when I checked in at London airport, as I so frequently continued to do. Next, I was off to Ireland, where I made two films in partnership with Oliver Unger.

For the first film, I had secured the rights from the widow of the English writer, Sax Rohmer, to his famous creation *Fu Manchu*. In this, the first of five *Fu Manchu* films I was to make, I had signed Christopher Lee as the famous villain, with Nigel Green as his opponent, Nayland Smith.

For the second subject, to be filmed back to back in Dublin, we lined up a remake of the Agatha Christie classic *Ten Little Indians*. Despite the Irish location, I borrowed the mountaintop setting of Christie's most recent success: *The Mouse Trap*. Our film was placed on an Austrian mountain top.

We signed a memorable cast, consisting of Hugh O'Brian, Stanley Holloway, Dennis Price, Fabian, Wilfred Hyde-White, Leo Genn, Shirley Eaton, Daliah Lavi, Marianne Hoppe and Mario Adorf.

For *The Face of Fu Manchu* we chose Kilmainham goal as our principal Dublin location. Unfortunately, our location manager stabled the mules we used in the film, in the condemned cells.

These were and will be forever associated with the Irish martyrs shot during the 1917 revolution. The Kilmainham Jail Committee, with whom we had made our deal, had a strong IRA element. We found our set piece location was invaded by two, heavily built laborers, who placed a plank across the camera tracks.

"It'll cost you a thousand pounds to remove it" I was told.

An adjournment to the local pub and an ample supply of Guinness provided an alternate solution—one hundred pounds in cash.

The finale of *The Face of Fu Manchu* was set in Tibet and we were able to recruit the substantial number of Oriental extras from the many Chinese medical students at Trinity College.

The two films I had produced in Ireland opened in the US with considerable success, thanks, in a large part, to the ideas developed by a brilliant publicist, soon to become, himself, a successful producer, Ed Feldman. The premier of *The Face of Fu Manchu* in New York coincided with a mayoral campaign and Ed plastered the subway with admonitions, aided by a giant poster of Christopher Lee, in costume, to "VOTE FOR FU MANCHU."

For *Ten Little Indians*, Ed interrupted the final minutes of the film, with a sixty second interval, to give the audience an opportunity to predict "WHO DUN IT."

My next move was to Morocco, with a script I had written, *Our Man in Marrakesh*. The cast was headed by Tony Randall, Terry Thomas, Senta Berger, Herbert Lom, Margaret Lee and for the first time of many, Klaus Kinski. We stayed at and shot much of the film, in the famous and really beautiful Mamounia Hotel. In the first week, Klaus distinguished himself by publicly urinating in the bar. He was asked to leave.

We managed to find a room for Klaus at another, slightly less luxurious hotel, but by the end of another week, he repeated the same behavior in the bar of the new hotel. We were out of season and there was only one other hotel open then in Marrakech, which was a much more humble establishment, catering usually for commercial travelers.

Yet again, Klaus disgraced himself and was asked to leave.

Klaus was required for another week on this location—what to do—where could he stay? I met with the three hotel managers and got them to agree that each one would accommodate Klaus for two days only. I still loved Klaus and he made half a dozen more films for me in the years to come.

I returned to London to produce my next two films, another Edgar Wallace thriller *Circus of Fear* and my second Sax Rohmer novel *The Brides of Fu Manchu*.

Then I lined up three projects in the Far East, based on Hong Kong, which I had first visited years ago in my radio days. We made Sax Rohmer's *Sumuru* with Shirley Eaton, Frankie Avalon and Wilfred Hyde-White, yet another Fu Manchu film; *The Vengeance of Fu Manchu* with, of course, Christopher Lee and Tsai Chin and thirdly, *Five Golden Dragons* starring Robert Cummings, with guest stars, including George Raft and Brian Donlevy.

Whilst Maria Rohm was busy starring in all of these three films in Hong Kong, I simultaneously embarked on another big production in Ireland:

Jules Verne's *Rocket to the Moon"* with Burl Ives, Terry Thomas, Lionel Jeffries, Gert Fröbe, Dahlia Lavi and Dennis Price.

The film was directed by Don Sharp and my partners were, AIP, (American International Pictures) whose founder and chairman, Sam Arkoff, became one of my most valued friends.

I was still unable to visit the United States but a telephone conversation with Sam ending with his wonderful and inimitable summary: "Good deal," meant that, without a shadow of a doubt, I was on the way to make another movie. I found that commuting between Ireland and Hong Kong was a considerable strain, but I had a great ally in Maria.

One time, when I was arriving in Hong Kong, late at night—that was before the tunnel was built and one had to cross by boat—I learned from Maria that our production manager was a thief and collected payoffs from the local artists and suppliers as a condition for them to get the job.

The next morning, on the ferry back from Kowloon, I explained to the dishonest man, that his services were no longer needed. Later on, that same morning, when Maria got to the set—the news had spread to the rest of the unit—there was a prolonged burst of applause, which was well deserved. In Hong Kong, I also developed a long term friendship with the head of the studio, Sir Run Run Shaw and his then publicist, who later became his impresario rival, Raymond Chow and his Mandarin speaking, American associate, Andre Morgan.

The films I produced in Hong Kong all qualified as British for, quite apart from the cast, which we had brought from London, the local crew and supporting cast, including the extras, were all residents of a British Crown Colony. When the British Unions objected, I pointed out to them and to the Board of Trade, and then the British Ministry that Run Run Shaw alone was making at least twenty pictures a year in Hong Kong and that, if I became the co-producer, these too could qualify as British.

There were no further objections.

As Maria was busy working on a movie in Hong Kong, I was making *Rocket to the Moon* and I needed another great looking actress. I found her in Germany. Her name was Renata Holt but I believe her real name was the Baroness Renate Von Holtzschu. She came to London to see me. While I was reading the script, I noticed that Renata had started to remove her makeup.

I realized that the lady was not of a mind to read the script. My guess was right. Renate started to talk about her life with her guardian. He was a substantially older man and he took a great interest in his young wards sex life. With his consent, she had recently gone to Paris, staying at a hotel on the Champs Elysées and worked as a street walker.

I found this all rather sad. When she asked me, I gave her the name of a Bordello, named Madame Kitty's, one of the few Bordello's left, in Paris. The reason this one was still open was because the Mayor of Paris was a regular customer there. The establishment could also be used for entertaining visiting diplomats. Renata had a very successful time there and it was through her that I met Madame Claude. In her day, Madame Claude was the most famous Madame in the world. Not only did she cater to visitors to Paris, including myself, but provided escorts for most of the rich people in Europe, as well as the entire Saudi Arabian Royal Family.

Here is another story involving Madame Claude.

I was in Rome and I thought I might like a drink, so I visited a bar not far from the hotel. There was a very attractive girl, seated, discussing something with a rather unpleasant looking gentlemen.

This bar was mainly populated with aging French prostitutes, who had come to Italy, to continue their careers. I asked to meet this young lady and, in those days, the gentlemen's and the ladies restrooms, where opposite each other, with a small lobby between them.

I met the attractive girl in the lobby between the washrooms. There she told me that she was a Swedish secretary, who had come to Italy on a vacation, with an older girl. The older girl had gone home and the younger one had stayed on. She was being looked after by an Italian boy who was a pimp.

He had used her to work in the nightclubs of Rome. I really felt sorry for her. I saw how unhappy she was. I suggested she leave her unpleasant companion and come with me. Well to make a long story short, I told her that if this was what she was going to do, there was a much better place to do it. I gave her the money for a ticket to Paris and the telephone number of Madame Claude.

Madame Claude received her with great enthusiasm. I kept in touch whenever I went to Paris. After some time, I saw the Swedish girl again and when I asked her, "You must be making quite a lot of money, what are you doing with it all?"

She replied that she was sending it back to her 'pimp' friend in Rome. "He is keeping it safe for me and, one day, we are going to live in the South of France."

I felt this to be utterly tragic, but I guess in the end we all have to live our own lives with our own individual abilities and karma.

So much for Madame Claude.

On one of my trips I also visited the Philippines and made a deal with the ex-Minister of Finance and imported a Philippine action star, Tony Ferrer, to join the cast of *The Vengeance of Fu Manchu*. In an action sequence, I had my first taste of and look at "Kung Fu." Our editor in London was not impressed.

"Harry," he warned me, "the audience is going to laugh at all those grunts and groans and peculiar acrobatics."

So we cut the sequence out of the film. Goes to show what we knew.

Some time later, when Run Run Shaw came to visit me at my London abode, he told me about a new discovery, Bruce Lee and his plans to produce a whole series of "Kung Fu" films. Run Run invited me to become his co-producer.

I was afraid, remembering my editor's comments, I turned the offer down.

Ultimately, I believe that it was Raymond Chow, the ex-publicist, who benefited most from the following "Kung Fu" boom.

You can't win them all.

My next venture took me to Madrid, with another script I had co-written and designed to star AIP's resident villain, Vincent Price, a most wonderful man. The movie was *House of a Thousand Dolls* also starring George Nader and Martha Hyer.

I had already set up my next project in Spain, entitled *Eve*.

An attractive American model, I'd met in Cannes, Celeste Yarnell, played the female Tarzan. The rest of the cast included Robert Walker Jr., Christopher Lee, Fred Clark, and Maria.

We were into our third week of filming near Madrid, when disaster struck—our Completion Guarantor went bankrupt.

I gathered the cast and crew and broke the news to them that I could pay them for their services to date, but then we would have to put them on suspension, whilst I worked on raising the finance with a new Completion Guarantor.

I was so relieved when everybody agreed, including Celeste, whose manager and husband was ever so much more concerned with the credits then if we could finish the film. Whatever happened, he wanted my assurance that Celeste's name would be in a box above the title.

I went to Brazil, where I had visited some years before and had maintained my contacts, in the hope of raising the money to complete the film. I was successful and am glad to say that, with the help of Sam Arkoff, I completed the arrangements and we resumed shooting. We checked into the Oro Verde Hotel on Copacabana beach and the cast and crew assembled for a welcoming reception.

When I noted that ten different nationalities were being represented, I remarked to Maria: "Who would believe it—another British picture is on its way."

The next problem presented itself in no time. Celeste, whose role required her to swing, in Tarzan fashion, from tree to tree, confessed that she suffered from vertigo—What to do now? We found a couple of excellent stunt doubles, swinging through the treetops, while Celeste was very busy modeling for stills.

Whist in Madrid I had struck up a friendship with a young Spanish director, Jesus Franco, known as Jess. Jess had just made a very successful picture *Necronomicon* to which Sam Arkoff had added the words "Look it up in Webster's" for the American release.

I brought Jess to Brazil to make two more pictures. Another Fu Manchu and a second Sumuru film *The Girl From Rio* with the inimitable George Sanders. Jess turned out to be a very imaginative and fast director when in a good mood. Sometimes though, Jess could be too fast for his own good and overuse the zoom lens. The finale of *The Girl From Rio* took place during the carnival. Jess had been working so fast that he had completed the picture a whole week before the carnival began.

Not wanting to waste a week, I sat down and, over the weekend, wrote the screenplay for *99 Women*. I was inspired by the recent hit *Papillon*, but told the story of three prison inmates in a savage women's prison, on a tropical island, off the cost of South America.

Casting three actresses already in Brazil, including Maria, Eliza Montés, from Spain, and Valentina Godoy, a native Brazilian actress, we could utilize the extra week.

Jess, with the same crew and the remaining negative, completed thirty minutes of action escape footage in five days in the Brazilian jungle. The footage was excellent. Jess at his most inspired. When, back in Paris, I showed the half hour footage to Oliver Unger and his partner, Harold Goldman. As we were walking down the Champs Elysées, Harold remarked in his inimitable fashion: "Harry, I smell money" and as always when it was about money, Harold was right. He had a sixth sense.

We added Herbert Lom to the cast as the sadistic and rapacious prison governor, Academy Award Winner, Mercedes MacCambridge, for the sadistic, lesbian governess and Maria Schell, for the soft hearted prison visitor.

We completed *99 Women* in three more weeks, in Alicante, Spain. The film opened within three months in the US and became the top grossing movie, in the Variety Box Office Chart, for a number of weeks.

That year, at the Cannes Film Festival, we had something to celebrate—not only the success of *99 Women*, but also the expansion of Oliver's company, Commonwealth United Entertainment—a really memorable occasion.

The chief financial backer, the entrepreneur of IOS fame, Bernie Cornfeld, together with his five current beauties, was the host for a truly lavish party, which occupied the entire old casino. Other stars in attendance, currently working for CUE Films (shooting was suspended for two days) included, Peter Sellers, Charlton Heston, Joseph Cotton, Peter Ustinov and many more.

A very glamorous party, it may have been the last in the true, old Hollywood style. It ended with a grand firework display, culminating with the initials C U E in scintillation flames. Maria was in seventh heaven and, very sweetly, thanked Oliver for "the fireworks."

Harry's mother Margaret with an inscription by Harry's father, Christmas 1916

Harry's mother Margaret during the First World War

Harry Alan Towers in 1921

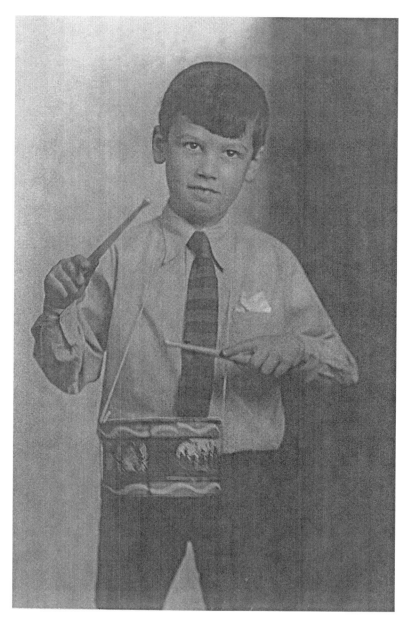

Harry Alan Towers in 1928

Harry Alan Towers, again in 1928

Harry Alan Towers on stage as a child actor, 1930, at age 9

Harry Alan Towers on stage as a child actor, 1931, at age 10

Harry Alan Towers (left) of the British Broadcasting Company of London pictured with Stanley W. Higginson, Warner Bros. managing director for Australia and Mrs. Higginson. This is the coupe's first visit to the tremendous Warner Bros Studios in Hollywood, in the offices of the STUDIO International Department. (ca. 1947)

Maria Rohm, Harry's wife, in her first stage
appearance, 1949, at age 4

Harry Alan Towers writing on a train, 1955

Christopher Lee and Harry Alan Towers on the set
of *Face of Fu Manchu*, 1965.
Photo: Karl Bayer

Harry Alan Towers and the Tower Bridge in London, 1965,
Photo: Karl Bayer

Daliah Lavi, Shirley Eaton, Hugh O'Brian, Leo Genn, Wilfred Hyde-White,
Dennis Price, Stanley Holloway and Mario Adorf on the set of Agatha Christie's
Ten Little Indians, 1965

Harry Alan Towers and Douglas Wilmer as Sir Dennis Nayland Smith, on the set of *The Brides of Fu Manchu* in Dublin, 1966

Robert Cummings, Rupert Davies and Maria Rohm
in *Five Golden Dragons*, 1967

Maria Rohm and James Darren in *Venus in Furs,* 1969
Photo: Simon Lopez

Ken Annakin (director) and Harry Alan Towers on the set
of *Call of the Wild* in Oslo, Norway, 1972

Partial cast and crew photo on *Shape of Things to Come*, 1979, with Jack Palance next to Harry Alan Towers

Angie Dickinson as Belinda McNair, Rod Steiger as Soapy Smith and Lorne Greene as Sam Steele in Jack London's *Klondike Fever*, 1980

Angie Dickinson as Belinda McNair in Jack London's *Klondike Fever*, 1980

Rod Steiger as Soapy Smith and Jeff East as Jack London
in *Klondike Fever*, 1980

Lorne Greene as Sam Steele in Jack London's *Klondike Fever*, 1980

Gordon Pinsent, Robin Gammell, Peter Carter (director), Harry Alan Towers (producer), Gilbert Taylor (Producer) (and unknown last man) at the press conference of *Klondike Fever* at the Genie Awards in Toronto, Canada, 1980.
Photo: Rick Porter

Shelley Winters as Mrs. Cole in *Fanny Hill,* 1983
Photo by John Paul, Scope Features

Ilya Salkind (son of Alexander Salkind) with companion
and Harry Alan Towers, ca. 1995

On the occasion of the Visit of Her Majesty Queen Elizabeth II
and
His Royal Highness The Prince Philip, Duke of Edinburgh
The British Ambassador
is commanded by The Queen to invite

Mr Harry A. Towers

to a Reception to be held at the Yusupov Palace,
Moika Naberezhnaya 94, St. Petersburg,
on Wednesday, 19th October, 1994 at 9.30 p.m.

Harry Alan Towers' invitation on his 74th birthday to meet Queen Elizabeth II
in St. Petersburg, Russia, where Harry was shooting *Bullet to Beijing*
with Michael Caine as Harry Palmer.

Chapter Eight
Let's Make More Movies

O ne year later to the day, I was again in Cannes and, passing by the Carlton Hotel terrace around 9 a.m., I saw the sole 'survivor' of CUE, Macgregor Scott, consoling himself with a single cup of coffee. I joined him and he told me, with a heavy heart, that this years' accommodations consisted of a single suite only—last night Macgregor's credit card was refused—and today, he found the door to the suite locked, plus, this was before Fax machines were in common use, the Telex in L.A. did not respond.

That's show business! Here today and gone tomorrow. Come to think of it, so is life.

This is another incident that shook me up quite a bit.

Leo Lax, a very valued French associate of mine—a wartime member of the French resistance—he now ran a dubbing studio in Paris. It was my habit to have dinner with Leo just before Cannes started. On this occasion, Leo drove me to a restaurant I was not familiar with, in a district I had never visited before. We had an enjoyable dinner and Leo drove me back to the hotel. When leaving for Nice the next morning, I realized I had left my overcoat, which Maria had just bought me for Christmas, at the restaurant the night before.

I had forgotten the name and address of the place, but I decided not to call and wake Leo so early I could do that later, when Leo would still have a chance to pick my coat up, before coming to the Cannes Festival.

It was not to be—Leo suffered a massive heart attack that day and alas died. Thus I lost another friend. The overcoat, which was so important a moment ago, did not matter so much anymore. Things are replaceable, people are not.

Alexander Salkind, who was famous for his creative ingenuity, was another regular visitor to Cannes in those days. Alexander has been producing since the end of WWII and his latest project was *Superman*.

For many years, the sky over Cannes was enlivened by an ever growing fleet of banner planes flying billboards, announcing that "Superman is Coming."

It was rumored that distributors, who had long since put up advance financing, would sing in unison: "One day our prints will come."

When, later on, Salkind got involved in an expensive remake of *The Three Musketeers*, he quietly changed the word "Film" to "Project" in all contracts pertaining to the films.

The cast of stars was very surprised, when they discovered, at the Royal Charity Premiere, that they had also shot a sequel *The Four Musketeers* that was coming soon. In other words, they had all made two films for the fee of one, without any of the highly paid lawyers catching that subtle change.

Alexander and I had also known each other during less prosperous days, when his home in Paris was the only security for a personal loan. At one time, Alex wanted to buy *Five Golden Dragons* for a client in Italy. Alex came to the screening, with his client, who looked a little forbidding. I later learned that one of his claims to fame was that he had collected on a Letter of Credit by filling the tin cans with stones and sand instead of film.

After viewing the film, we agreed on a price of $35,000, with 10% down and the balance in a Letter of Credit, payable upon delivery.

For the down payment I received a cheque, which I couldn't cash for quite some time. The Letter of Credit was from a bank in Zug, Switzerland, which did not look to confidence inspiring. When, almost a year later, I ran into temporary money trouble on another film, I was looking through my papers and found the above mentioned LC. I asked the production accountant to go to the bank in Zug and present the LC, to be paid, in cash, by the close of business, or else he was instructed to call the "Carabinieri."

Happy to say, the accountant came back with the money and all was well.

Some time later, in the Casino in Cannes, I met Oliver Unger who was accompanied by Alexander Salkind. Oliver introduced him to me.

"Oh, I know Harry," said Salkind, "I buy pictures from him,"

He adds, "And he always gets paid."

"I certainly do," was my polite response.

When my mother was still alive, I had acquired another apartment in a newly completed building, just around the corner, at 59.Devonshire Street. I continued to occupy Hallam Street, where Maria lived with me now. My mother was far from happy with the arrangement and would often walk around the corner, especially in the evening, rattling the letterbox and proclaiming, "This is Mrs. Towers of 84 Hallam Street and I demand to be let in at once."

Mother was not too happy either in the penthouse apartment where she now lived. She kept saying that the building was swaying. For the last six months I got her around the clock nurses, as her health was deteriorating. Alas, we lost her in 1968. Maria came with me to the funeral and I was able to show her our country cottage in Telscombe. After my mother's death, we gave up the Hallam Street apartment and moved to Devonshire Street.

The place was so full of memories and reminders of mother that, whilst in Berlin for the Film Festival, we decided to establish a residence there. Berlin, at that time, was a city dominated by young students and seniors and it was easy to find an apartment, suitable for our needs. As luck would have it, our good friend, Arthur Brauner, came to our aid. Arthur, a very prominent German film producer and owner of the CCC Studios since 1946, also owned many properties in Berlin. During the height of the Cold War, many businessmen were leaving the city and very anxious to sell their land.

After President Kennedy, in his famous speech, declared, "Ich bin ein Berliner," confidence was restored and Arthur became an even richer man.

We leased a magnificent penthouse from Arthur, on the famous Kurfúrstendamm, which has been largely rebuilt after being destroyed during the war. So we settled down, in the city that was really an island in the midst of, what was now, Eastern Europe. Maria had a good time decorating the apartment, which had an enormous living room and a magnificent view.

We enjoyed visiting the opera in East Berlin, although Maria, with her childhood memories in Russian occupied Vienna, was rather terrified when going through the check point. After some time, we moved back to London. Jess, who was our "in house" director at this time, was preparing for our next film, for which I had written the screenplay, the Marquis de Sade's *Justine*.

I had found Romina Power, the eighteen year old daughter of Tyrone Power and Linda Christian, for the title role and Maria played her worldly sister, Juliette.

We had a wonderful supporting cast—the great character actor and most charming Akim Tamiroff and Jack Palance, who was to continue working with me over a period of many years. I was very sorry when Jack died in November of 2006. We'll surely all miss him.

Justine was shot in Barcelona, where we were able to incorporate the uniquely distinctive architecture of the famous Spanish architect, Antoni Gaudi. Due to the strong influence of the Catholic Church in Spain at the time, our Spanish partners became concerned with the erotic content of the screenplay and withdrew from the co-production. I am still wondering what they were thinking the subject was about, when they agreed to the deal in the first place?

On top of that, attracted by the title, the Spanish Minister of Culture, while on a trip to Rome, went, incognito, to see the film. Naturally he recognized the architecture and, as a result, we also lost the Italian nationality, due to the co-production agreement.

Happily, the film was a great success in Germany.

When offering the part of the Marquis de Sade to Klaus Kinski, his agent demanded more money, for one day of shooting, than was available in the budget. I offered Klaus the alternative of half a day's work for half the money.

That clinched the deal.

We filmed Klaus as he was driven, in a coach, into the prison yard.

The next sequences were with Klaus sitting in different positions at a desk, writing into his diary, whilst women in chains and various degrees of nudity, provided the background, together with the narrative that accompanied the story.

The German distributor ignored everybody else in the large and distinguished cast and publicized the film as: "KLAUS KINSKI as the Marquis de Sade in *Justine*." It took some time before Klaus forgave me.

Meantime, Jess directed another Fu Manchu film, *The Castle of Fu Manchu*. Not his best work, but I am half to blame for that.

Massimo Dallamano, a great Italian cameraman *Fistful of Dollars* had now also started to direct.

I had had the idea of re-making Oscar Wilde's classic tale *The Picture of Dorian Gray* but update it to the swinging sixties. Luchino Visconti had just directed *The Damned* and introduced us to his new discovery, the young Austrian actor Helmut Berger. I thought he would be perfect for the role.

Around Helmut I assembled an excellent cast: Herbert Lom, as Henry Wooton, (immortalized by George Sanders in the definitive version of *Dorian Gray* with Hurd

Hatfield as Dorian) and Richard Todd played the painter of the portrait in our version. We filmed *Dorian* in Rome, Hamburg and London.

The young ingénue, who kills herself, was played by Marie Liljedahl, a young Swedish actress who had already worked for me in de Sade's *Philosophy in the Boudoir* directed by Jess, also starring Maria.

The film enjoyed considerable success in the US and elsewhere, under the title *Eugenie*.

In the meantime, Jess was directing yet another film for us, in Portugal, *The Bloody Judge* played by Christopher Lee, inspired by the notorious Judge Jeffries. I continued my association with Jess by fulfilling Christopher Lee's ambition, to go back to Bram Stoker's original *Dracula* story.

We returned to Barcelona for the principal photography and invited Herbert Lom to join the cast, playing Van Helsing. We still had to find an actor for the mad Renfield, who's confined to an insane asylum on a diet of flies.

Klaus Kinski was the obvious choice, but he refused the part, claiming that he was opposed to appearing in a *Dracula* film. After a long talk with Klaus's agent, we decided to send him only his part of the script, without any title. We shot his scenes, separate from the rest of the film, in Italy.

Maria, playing the ingénue role, was in the scene with Klaus, where he almost succeeded in strangling her, in the film. The situation was complicated by the fact that Klaus kept asking Maria if she was sure he was not appearing in a *Dracula* movie. Being loyal to me, as always, Maria insisted that Klaus was mistaken and we finally completed the scenes.

During our shooting of Anne Sewell's *Black Beauty* with Mark Lester, the juvenile star of *Oliver* and Walter Slezak, Maria, who played Lady Anne, broke six ribs when falling off her horse while practicing to ride side-saddle for the part. After one week in hospital, Maria, bravely, got back on the horse to continue her role and complete the film. That's what I call a real trooper.

Meantime, I started preparing another picture in Spain, again with Mark Lester, called *Night Hair Child* which also starred Brit Ekland, who, seventeen years later would portray Mariella Novotny in the film *Scandal*.

I could never have thought that at this time.

Lilly Palmer, who I knew well from my television days, when she had hosted the *Lilli Palmer Playhouse* for me, played a cameo role. Ms. Palmer was, at that time, married to Rex Harrison, who was starring in London's West End in *Bell, Book and Candle*, also known as "Bell, Book and Kendall" due to the fact that Rex was heavily involved with another actress, Kay Kendall.

I had, first, met Kay during the war, when she was a hostess at the Stage Door Canteen. Kay was the brilliant star of the memorable comedy film *Genevieve* and *Les Girls* among others. Kay and Rex fell in love when appearing together in *Marriage A La Mode* in 1955.

When Rex realized that Kay was suffering from leukemia, he divorced Lilli Palmer and married Kay in 1957 and they stayed together until her death at the young age of thirty-three in 1959.

Nat Cohen, the head of Anglo Amalgamated Productions, a long term friend and trusted business partner would give me his answers immediately.

We immortalized the deals on a single sheet of paper, drafted by my lawyer, Tristram Owen, who was a firm believer in the theory that any longer document was, potentially, not necessarily an agreement, but a possible source of litigation. Tristram was the best lawyer I have ever known, bar none.

One day, in his office, Nat tossed a book at me, entitled *My Family and Other Animals*, a best seller by Gerald Durrell. Nat had been trying to realize this project for quite a long time, without success and was asking me now, to have a go. My first move was a trip to the home of Gerald Durrell, on the Channel Islands, where, to my surprise and amazement, he had his own personal zoo.

Christopher Miles, the older brother of the Oscar nominated British actress, Sarah Miles, was already committed to the project. Together, we set off to Corfu, where the action in the book took place. We found all the locations we needed and got all the necessary permissions. I had already approached Ingrid Bergman, to play the mother and, after a very pleasant lunch at the Connaught Hotel in London, she'd agreed.

I spent another wonderful afternoon with Ingrid Bergman, at her home in Paris, together with her friend, Claudette Colbert. Both were so beautiful and so charming— a true delight!

But, as so often, there was a problem. Unbeknownst to me, Chris had agreed to direct another film and was no longer available. I suppose we all have to survive as we think best. I proposed Nicolas Roeg, to Nat Cohen. As the two had never met, we all got together. Whilst Nick was very interested in the project, he explained to Nat that he had a prior commitment.

Nat bridled aggressively, "Who with"?

"Cadbury's Chocolate," Nick replied. "They paid the rent, when you didn't call."

We never made the movie. I was sorry, but I had a busy year ahead of me anyway.

The BBC made a *My Family and Other Animals* TV Series in the late eighties and a TV movie in 2005.

The year 1972 was an eventful and fruitful year. I produced two major movies:

Jack London's *Call of the Wild* with Charlton Heston and Michelle Mercier was the first.

The very talented Ken Annakin (*The Magnificent Men in Their Flying Machines*) was directing the film in Norway. In Norway, the guidelines for the treatment of animals were so strict that for the scenes with an exhausted dog we had to move across the border to Sweden.

When I apologised to Charlton Heston for the inconvenience, his response was, "I understand, Harry. It's a pity that the dog is the star of the picture and not myself."

Unfortunately he was all too right.

Simultaneously, in Spain, I filmed Robert Louis Stevenson's *Treasure Island* with Orson Welles, Walter Slezak and Lionel Stander. Orson had originally planned to direct the same subject, back to back with *Chimes at Midnight*, but, as I have mentioned before, often, life does not work out the way we planned it.

Man proposes—God disposes.

After I explained to Orson that, if he were to direct, I would have real difficulty getting a Completion Guarantor, he reluctantly agreed to accept my choice for the top-notch director, John Hough, a man I respected and trusted completely.

Essential for *Treasure Island* was a pirate ship

I'd found a suitable vessel, the *Hispaniola*, which was moored in the Thames and used as a restaurant. We bought the ship and hired a three men crew of experienced Channel Islanders, to take it to the location in Almeria, Spain.

I got a phone call, in the middle of the night, from my Spanish partner and long time friend, Andres Vicente Gomez: "Our ship has drowned" he told me.

My first concern was the crew who, luckily, had been able to save themselves, but the ship, alas, had sunk during a storm in the Bay of Biscay.

We had only two weeks to find a replacement and we succeeded.

Orson was not an easy man to work with. One day, during the shooting, he had an argument with John, who left the set. As we were filming aboard the 'new' Hispaniola, Orson realized the predicament he had caused, so he got into a boat and rowed off in pursuit of John. They both came back and all went well between them after that.

During the shooting, however, Orson was reluctant to spend time on satisfactory sound recording, proclaiming that in any event, he would have to post sync his role, with Squire Trelawney being played by Walter Slezak, from Vienna and Billy Bones brought to life by Lionel Stander, from the Bronx.

"I shall give you an authentic, Southern England accent" he declared in his unforgettable voice.

With Principal Photography complete, it proved difficult to pin Orson down, but he finally agreed to make himself available in Paris.

One of the conditions was that the looping sessions start at midnight, with an ample supply of French red wine available. Some time later, my long time editor, Nicholas Wentworth, complained that he could not understand one word of what Orson was saying.

The film was due to open, in the US, within a matter of weeks. We had, therefore, no alternative but to go ahead with Orson's voice anyway. However, Nat Cohen, the British Distributor and our American television licensees, insisted that Orson do his re-voicing again.

When Orson failed to show up at the insistence of the Completion Guarantors, the role was re-voiced by Robert Rietti, a past master of imitation. Alas, some years ago, I had to admit, that the voice on the soundtrack is a good imitation and not the unmistakable real thing.

During the years that followed, I continued to keep in touch with Orson and his trials and tribulations. Finally, through a series of very successful advertisements for a major American winery, Gallo, Orson achieved, at last, some financial stability.

It is somehow ironic that this gifted man, multi-talented in a number of arts, could not find financial success earlier in his life. I believe he was just ahead of his time.

I wanted to make a mini-series *The World of H.G Wells with Orson Welles*. I couldn't reach Orson by phone, so I sent him this fax: "Orson—where the hell are you—Welles?"

The following day I picked up the phone: "This is Orson—where the hell are you—Welles?" came the ever unique and captivating voice. I did not know it, but this was the last time we ever spoke together during his life.

Some time earlier, when producing *Eugenie* in Spain, I had paid off the supporting cast with personal cheques. I found out later, that one of the cheques had "bounced," which is a very serious offence in Spain.

I called Vicente, my co-producer and friend, and asked him to pay off the actor from the funds he was currently holding for my account.

Unfortunately, Vicente failed to do so, which led to another very unpleasant experience for me. Late one evening there was a knock on my hotel room door in Madrid.

It was the Hotel Night Manager, accompanied by a Spanish police officer, with a warrant for my arrest. I had no idea what this was all about, but needless to say, I felt like I was having a nightmare. I was escorted downstairs and placed in the back of a police car and driven to the nearby police station. All kinds of thoughts were running rampant through my mind. It did not help that upon needing to go to the toilet, I discovered to my horror, that there was just a deep pit in the ground.

Talk of feeling insecure—now physically as well as emotionally.

I was finger-printed, questioned and conveyed, in the company of other prisoners, to the Madrid House of detention. I must say, I found it to be an improvement on the Tombs in New York, but most everything would be. I had managed to call Vicente and make him aware of my plight.

Whilst awaiting my release, I took the advantage of attending Mass in the Catholic chapel of the prison, for the first and only time, for I am Church of England myself. I found the experience very soothing—I felt uplifted, not so forlorn and isolated, in the presence of a higher power. I had, as yet, not told Maria, I didn't want to worry her, I was definitively worried enough for the both of us.

Vicente was very sorry about his oversight in the matter. He was able to arrange my release after a few days, having paid the debt and, he also made sure, that the unfortunate incident was deleted from public record.

We had a stiff drink together and I forgave him for his negligence and boarded a flight to Oslo, Norway.

Chapter Nine
Some Call it Euro-pudding

On my arrival I had to deal with yet another challenging situation. I was expecting the arrival of the villain for *Call of the Wild*, who was being provided by the Italian co-producer of the film, who was also a long time friend and great supporter of mine, Giulio Sbariga., more about him in a moment.

In those days the Italian Film Industry was booming. Due to their lower costs, they had triumphed, over Hollywood, in producing B action features, the so called "Spaghetti Westerns."

They did recruit a number of American television actors, most notably Clint Eastwood in Sergio Leone's *For a Fistful of Dollars*. An increasing number of Italian actors had adopted pseudonyms, such as Bud Walker and Terence Hill, or they could be combination names of Hollywood stars, such as "Tyron Gable" or Clark Power." The actor we were waiting for was called, George Eastman.

When I met George after his arrival, it was instantly clear that this actor belonged to the latter group; he did not speak one word of English. I should have discussed that with Giulio beforehand, but I thought it was understood, that some English was required. With the help of my interpreter, my great and indispensable stills photographer, Pierluigi, I welcomed George in Italian and greeted his very attractive blond wife, who was also an actress. "Miss Kim Kodak, I assume," was my immediate response.

Pierluigi dissolved into laughter—at least somebody appreciated the joke.

Giulio Sbariga ran Fono Roma, the vast post-production facility, which complimented CineCitta, an equally vast studio. Both were part of Mussolini's grandiose plans for the Italian Film industry. In those happy days, Italy was churning out around four hundred films per year. All their films, both big and small, would all too frequently run out of money during the post-production. Thus, Giulio ended up with a stake, big or small, in nearly every picture that used Fono Roma for their post-production house.

Call of the Wild turned out to be a great success in Italy and spawned a succession of copy-cats, nicknamed "Spaghetti Westerns in the Snow."

I, myself, helped Giulio produce one of them named *Call of the Wolf*, starring Jack Palance and Joan Collins.

I knew Joan, since the exciting days and nights, when I was running ATV. I had featured Joan and Jackie, her sister the writer, on a late night talk show. After the show was over, I took the two teenage girls out for a night on the town and we had a lot of laughs.

The last time I saw Giulio was aboard a plane, en route from Rome to Nice, for the Cannes Film Festival. When Giulio told me that he was going to be in Cannes for one day only, I asked what the reason was for his short stay. He replied, "It's just time enough for me to walk down the Croisette and back to the Martinez, so that my friends or enemies can say—ah—the old bastard is still alive."

I am still going to Cannes myself every year, as I've been doing for over forty years. I am increasingly tempted to emulate Giulio and "keep it short."

In 1973, I found fresh fields to conquer. I was approached by the Iranian Producers Association, to go to Iran to make a film. My co-producer there was the perfect gentleman, a gem of a man, Nuri Ashtiani. I secured the rights to remake Agatha Christie's timeless mystery: *Ten Little Indians* under its alternate title, *And Then There Were None*. I adapted the story, so that it took place in a luxury hotel, near the ruins of the city of Persepolis, which was destroyed by Alexander the Great. I was able to get a great international cast: Oliver Reed, Elke Sommer, Richard Attenborough, Stéphane Audran, Charles Aznavour, as well as two veterans from the James Bond movies, Gert Fröbe and Adolfo Celi and, of course, Maria Rohm. We shot most of the film in Persepolis and the famous and aesthetically gorgeous Shah Abbas Hotel in Isfahan, where the cast and principal crew where also staying.

One night, during a party in the basement night club, Oliver, while dancing with Maria, became involved in a fight with the director, Peter Collinson, who, shall we say had a lot of issues of a challenging nature. I knew that Peter had been in the Actor's Orphanage when he was a child. Noël Coward was the CEO at that time. No doubt, this connection helped Peter cast Noël as a lead in *The Italian Job* that Peter directed.

Now Richard Attenborough was the head of the Actor's Orphanage.

When a feud developed between Peter Collinson and Oliver Reed is was Dickie who did his best to mediate. Olly's body guard, Reg Prince beat up a bodyguard of the Shah of Iran. The films Spanish crew got into the fight as well and there were some injuries that required stitches, and the cost of the destroyed night club was not inconsiderable. Oliver had to leave the hotel, but the rest stayed on and finished the film.

Toward the end of production we started to run short of money. In order to settle our debts and get the cast and crew safely out of Iran and on their way home, I managed with difficulty, to raise the funds but had to fly to Tehran to receive them.

Unfortunately, the Iranian religious holidays were about to commence and the bank was crowded and the staff unhelpful. With my British Passport, I penetrate deep inside the bank's security zone and succeeded in explaining to a friendly manager my urgent problem.

After an hour's wait, he brought me the money: one hundred thousand American dollars, in cash. I put the money in a paper bag and set off on a long walk through the crowded streets of Teheran, to the offices of a trusted Armenian Travel Agent, who had been recommended to me by Armenian born Charles Aznavour, who was among the stars of the film.

I arrived safely with the money.

The travel agent was horrified and stated: "There must have been a hundred Iranian thieves in the streets who might have murdered you for that money."

"Maybe I was lucky," was my response.

I want to mention that there have been a number of omissions of the movies I have produced, including *Venus in Furs* that was largely shot in Istanbul, with James Darren and Maria. I went on to make a number of less memorable films, mainly in Italy, before I returned to the Far East.

I had written a story about a young girl, who arrived with an older man, ostensibly her guardian, but actually her lover. When the man gets arrested, the young girl finds herself alone and unprotected in Hong Kong. I called the story, provisionally, *The End of Innocence*.

Massimo Dellamano had agreed to direct, but I still needed to find an eighteen year old actress for the lead.

In Paris I was introduced to a young actress, Annie Brilland, with short blond hair and the appearance of a street urchin. I flew her to Rome to meet Massimo, but she had started to irritate me already and I was thinking of sending her back to Paris. That ides changed when I saw the rather unexpected results of a photo session I had arranged for her with Pierluigi, one of the greatest still photographers of all time, whose classic production stills of Sophia Loren, Raquel Welch and Ursula Andres had helped to launch their careers. The stills were sensational!

I hurriedly cancelled her return flight to Paris, signed her for the film and renamed her Annie Belle. We left for Hong Kong

For her supposed guardian in the film, I'd signed one of the great American characters, locally known as the "Major of Rome," Charlie Fawcett. I had known him for many years.

Charlie was everybody's best friend. He excelled as a party giver, inviting beautiful young women and powerful, rich men. Charlie liked to help his friends and loved to bring people closer together, he was also always good for a laugh.

One typical example: Charlie had met another friend of mine, a former Miss America, who had been touring Europe to publicize a movie. When Charlie learned that the young lady was preparing to go back to the US, he suggested that maybe she would, first, care to visit Iran for the Tehran Film Festival and meet his 'good friend' the Shah of Iran.

The lady accepted the invitation, but only saw the Shah at a distance at the various receptions, until the day before she was planning to leave the country. She was, very politely, invited to join the Foreign Minister for tea.

Her fellow guest was the Shah, who insisted on showing the young beauty the VIP accommodation in the Ministry. One thing led to another and the young lady decided to stay another week, with daily 'conferences' at the Foreign Ministry.

It turned out that the lady left with a considerably larger wardrobe and an impressive collection of jewelry.

When the young lady and Charlie met again, in Rome, before her departure to the US, Charlie suggested that she might return to the US via Morocco, where the King of Morocco was his best friend.

When finally returning to the US, she was filling out the immigration card. When the question of occupation came up, she wrote down, after some consideration: "King Fucker."

I had decided that despite Annie's sometimes nerve-wrecking attitude, I wanted to sign her for three more films. I felt that she had good potential as an actress.

When back in Rome for post-production, an unexpected offer came our way.

Annie burst into my room and told me, with great excitement, that she had met an American producer, who wanted her to star in a film with Linda Lovelace, of *Deep Throat* renown, directed by Emmanuelle Arsan of *Emanuelle* fame.

I learned from the Italian co-producer, that there was a problem.

Having signed these two highly publicized names, they discovered that in a forthcoming Federal trial of her co-star in *Deep Throat*, Harry Reams, Linda Lovelace had agreed to give evidence for the prosecution and to protect herself, had decided that she could not appear in any erotic scenes.

The script had to be re-written, so that these scenes could be played by Annie Belle. As Annie's new Italian boyfriend, Al Clever, was also in the cast, Annie welcomed the opportunity.

After the deals were all done, we all left for Manila, where the film was to be shot. We were accompanied by a cute little mongrel dog, which Annie had adopted in Hong Kong and named Bobo. When I asked around if someone had lost their pet, the only answer I got, was that in Chinese eyes, Bobo was edible and that was all.

The filming had begun in the Philippines.

It transpired that Emmanuelle Arsan, who was billed as the director, was, in fact, a Eurasian starlet who's highly successful biography had been ghost written by her husband, Louis-Jacques Rollet-Andriane, a retired French diplomat. It was he who was to direct the film.

It soon became apparent that the situation would develop into a disaster.

After two weeks of filming, there had been very slow progress and, in addition to the inexperienced director, Linda Lovelace refused to go on the set, even if the sculpture on her desk was not fully clothed.

Maria had come out to support me, but developed a kidney problem.

Only Annie and Bobo appeared to be flourishing. Finally, the Italian co-producer came to me for advice.

"Either Emmanuelle or Linda have to go" he complained.

I recommended for Linda to go. "What shall I tell the press?" he asked.

"Just tell them," I suggested, "Linda ate someone who disagreed with her."

We finally did complete the film and returned to Rome.

At that time, I also had the eighteen years young Miss Teenage Germany under contract. I named her Ziggy Zanger.

Ziggy had made a film for me in Rome *Black Cobra* that starred Jack Palance. She was a very entertaining young girl who made lots of jokes that were extra funny, because of her broken English accent. Aboard a teetotal Saudi Arabian Airlines Flight, Ziggy, firmly declined a milk shake and insisted on an oil sheik.

Annie and Ziggy worked together in the film *Black Velvet – White Silk* a production I agreed to supervise in Egypt. The filming was to take place in Aswan on the Nile.

The director, Brunello Rondi, was a somewhat pompous Italian, one of the 'hangers on' of Federico Fellini. He wore riding breeches on the set, trying to look like Cecil B. De Mille.

On the third day of shooting, Brunello informed Ziggy, that he was a firm believer in the right of any director to have sex with any member of the cast.

To his delight, at first, Ziggy responded: "That's no problem."

Then she continued, "I've talked to the crew and they all agree that you're no director." Collapse of stout party.

Despite strict censorship in Egypt, *Black Velvet – White Silk* was very erotic for its day. The rushes were hand carried back to Rome every week and the representative of the Egyptian Censor, who was always on the set, was provided with a liberal supply of whiskey.

We were scheduled to complete the film in Cairo. This was the third film of three films to be made in Egypt, by my Italian co-producer. He had promised to provide the Egyptian studio with a second hand Italian film laboratory, in exchange for their services, but nothing had arrived.

On the last day of shooting, in Cairo, the police descended upon us and seized the Italian camera gear and the remaining negative.

Typically, if I may say so, the Italian Producer had sent the cast and crew to Egypt via Sudan Airways, which operated the route back to Rome, only once a week. We had five days to wait and no money.

I went to Cairo airport and made a deal with the local TWA representative. I would stand at the gate and give him one hundred dollars in cash for every endorsed Sudan Airways return coupon he accepted.

With cast and crew safely aboard, we left for Rome.

I felt thoroughly dejected until the Italian Production Manager, unexpectedly, informed me that the crew had smuggled aboard the plane, in their personal luggage, both the dismantled, Italian owned, camera, in bits and pieces, as well as, the last of the rushes. They had left the camera cases and tins of negative behind, filled with stones. I joined the toast to the indefatigable spirit of the crew.

For Annie Belle's next film which would prove to be our last together, I joined forces with Carlo Ponti to make *Night of the High Tide* that was to be shot in Martinique in the Caribbean and Montreal, as an Italian/Canadian co-production.

Anthony Steel was the male star and, alas too intimately involved with spirits of the drinking kind, quite unlike Pamela Grier who was professional and fun.

We had a very competent Italian director, Luigi Scattini, and the shooting in Martinique went smoothly.

We moved on to Montreal, which was to mark the beginning of a long association with Canada, where I had started my overseas connections in my radio days.

Night of the High Tide qualified as a Canadian co-production and for the newly available tax deferral financing advantage. I can still remember until this day Annie's constant repetition of the priorities in her life:

"We make something"

"We take taxi"

"We go shopping"

"I take pregnancy test."

I planned, but never completed a fifth film with Annie Belle.

The French title was *Entente Cordiale*, the English one *Closed Up Tight*. It co-starred Annie Belle with Marti Feldman who had been discovered by Mel Brooks, who had starred him in *Young Frankenstein*.

Everybody thought he was wearing elaborate makeup, but they were wrong. This was Marti Feldman's real face.

I also featured Tommy Trinder in the cast. I started with two weeks shooting an elaborate chase sequence in the deserted streets of Paris in late August. The sequence was orchestrated and directed by the same stunt supervisor who had acted in a similar capacity on all the earlier James Bond films. We publicised the film and made a number of presales, but not enough to finance the film. We had to abandon.

Somewhere in a vault in Paris lies the chase footage which we shot and which, ever since, has remained "closed up tight."

May you be happy dear Annie Belle—wherever you may be.

Once the film was completed, I had to concentrate on finding new Canadian investors interested in using the financing availability. I flew to Winnipeg, where I had arranged a meeting with a wonderful character, the Rabbi Nessis.

Nessis, formerly the Chief Rabbi of Western Canada, had fallen out with his flock and had been involved in bitter litigation, in which he had been represented by a charming Roman Catholic Queen's Counselor. When the Rabbi found himself out of a job, he decided to turn to a new profession, as the Organizer and Salesman for a Film Tax Shelter Company.

Night of the High Tide was to be the first such offering. We had a rocky and lengthy road ahead. Rabbi Nessis had a row with his Q.C., who returned all the cheques to the initial investors. After retrieving them again, we were ready to close the deal just before Christmas.

As we left the bank, after the closing, in cold and windy Winnipeg, I accidentally dropped a paper bag, filled with hundred dollar bills, which was the Rabbi's share of the deal. He hurriedly collected the scattered bills. When I suggested taking a taxi back to the hotel, he demurred at my suggestion and announced that there was a free bus we could take.

The Rabbi paid me, what I felt to be, the ultimate complement: "Harry," he said, "you would have made a good Rabbi."

I felt, despite the intended honor, I was not really suited to that vocation.

For a long time I had wanted to make a sequel to: "Rider Haggard's *King Solomon's Mines*, entitled *Allan Quartermain*.

My father had been a Rider Haggard fan and my middle name was derived from the misspelled version of the explorer's first name. After I completed the script and named it *King Solomon's Treasure*, I decided to make the film another Canadian Co-production, to be shot, partially, in South Africa. As these were still the days of apartheid, I chose to film with a South African/Canadian crew in independent Swaziland.

When the small Canadian crew arrived in the capital, Mbabane, the bus carrying us from the airport broke down. In the distance we could hear the roar of lions. I had to assure my terrified Canadian colleagues, that the roars came from a nearby and, totally enclosed, game reserve.

The cast of the film was headed by David McCallum, John Colicos, Brit Ekland and, we hoped, Terry Thomas. Unfortunately, to my distress, TT could not face up to the task and on his arrival in Johannesburg, asked me to replace him.

I managed to get Patrick Macnee of *Avengers* fame and after finishing the filming in Southern Africa, we returned to Montreal, where Wilfred Hyde-White joined the cast.

Around the time of the first *Star Wars* success, when Science Fiction was very popular, I felt that it was a good time to turn to the master and I adapted H. G. Wells's *The Shape of Things to Come* with Jack Palance. The film was shot entirely at the Kleinberg Studios, on the outskirts of Toronto.

For my next venture, we moved to British Columbia. Pierre Berton, who was born in Dawson City, became our advisor and I borrowed from him, the title *Klondike Fever*. Our story was based on the adventures of Jack London in the Klondike. For the young Jack, I cast Jeff East, who had played young Clark Kent in the Christopher Reeve *Superman* movie. Lorne Greene, a friend from my radio days, agreed to play Sam Steel, Rod Steiger was set for Soapy Smith and Angie Dickinson played the madam, who runs the saloon and, the British actor Barry Morse as John Thornton. Last, but by no means least, the truly fine Canadian actor, Gordon Pinsent and Robin Gammell completed the cast. Gordon was to win a Genie Award, the Canadian Oscar, for his work in the film.

At the tiny township of Wells, where we started filming, a small motel was the only accommodation available. Happily, we could persuade some of the local inhabitants to temporarily make parts of their homes available for our stars.

Our filming coincided with the Oscar ceremonies in Hollywood. Maria and I enjoyed a hilarious evening with commentary on the proceedings by Angie Dickinson and Rod Steiger, both of whom had had close relationships with some of the honored talent.

The filming took us all over British Columbia, including Harrison Hot Springs and Kamloops. On one of the car rides from Harrison Hot Springs to Vancouver, I was accompanied by Barry Morse. As a boy, in London, Barry had been an ardent music hall fan and could remember the "billing" of the best known stars of those days.

From my own experience, I too consider myself an expert on the subject and we ended up playing a fascinating game. We challenged each other, first to match the billing with the star and then, more difficult, the stars with the billing, i.e. Charles Penfold; *The Laughing Policeman*. One of the best car-rides I have ever had.

Some months later, we had a gala premiere in Edmonton, as part of the annual "Klondike Days" Festival. For the premier, the audience wore authentic period costumes.

Back in Europe, I came up with an idea for a new version of the classic tale of erotica, John Cleland's *Fanny Hill*. I met the Italian director, Tinto Brass, who had achieved some success with *Salon Kitty* and then gone on to direct *Caligula* for Bob Guccione, of *Penthouse*. They had a row and Bob, who had finished the film by himself, had become involved in litigation over Tinto's "author's rights."

I worked with Tinto for quite some time. I brought Tinto to London as well as Canada to find the locations and do the casting. The subject matter was in public domain and I suddenly learned, that Tinto planned to double cross me. He had entered into a partnership with Aurelio de Laurentis, nephew of Dino, and they planned to go ahead with the film, without me.

I'd already cast the title role with a young Canadian actress, Lisa Raines. I knew that Tinto was arriving in London at the beginning of the following week to finalize the locations. Rather upset, I set up a press conference and photo call at my apartment and introduced Lisa, costumed as Fanny Hill. I did this on a Saturday and the story and the pictures made every Sunday newspaper, in some cases, the front page.

Tinto and Aurelio were furious. They contacted the principal laboratories for information on our activities. Then a well known Italian lawyer contacted me, offering "to buy me off."

When I went to Rome, in my early days, as a film producer, I had some experience of Italian business practices and ethics. I discovered that, my then Italian partner had completed and released two of my best films, by duplicating the dubbing materials.

Well, life is about learning which I did and, after a while, I began to like doing business in Italy again. I came of age, in this respect, when Giulio Sbariga, who was known as the godfather, told me, one day, that I was known as the "King of Naples."

As most of the thieves in Italy are believed to be from that city, I appreciated the compliment. There is an old adage that "it takes a thief to catch a thief."

I put together the financing for our production of *Fanny Hill* and we started shooting in London, adding Shelley Winters to the cast, as a Madame, Wilfred Hyde-White as an elderly client and Oliver Reed, as a crooked lawyer.

Originally I had offered the role played by Wilfred Hyde White to his friend, Robert Morley, and reminded him of his oft quoted remark: "Never read a script, or refuse a part."

His response was: "My dear Harry, in this case I'll make an exception."

Gerry O'Hara directed, as well as collaborated on the new screenplay.

I had and have a long standing friendship with the uniquely talented English director, Ken Russell, which had started some years previously.

I had commissioned a screenplay from Melvyn Bragg, based on the life of Peter the Great. We had planned to star Oliver Reed in the title role, but it was not to be, as we could not raise the financing for the project.

Now, Ken approached me with a script he had co-written and owned, *The Beethoven Secret*, which dealt with the women in Beethoven's life.

It was an excellent script. I approached Anthony Hopkins for the title role. Before becoming an actor, Hopkins had aspired to be a pianist. He liked the script and agreed immediately.

For the women in Beethoven's life we lined up a wonderful cast. With the help of Ken we had Glenda Jackson, Charlotte Rampling and a seventeen year old Jodie Foster. We were to shoot the film in Vienna and Berlin.

The sets had been built and Anthony Hopkins had grown a beard for the role. I was one week before the start date for Principal Photography, when the financing collapsed. The Bank of Thurn and Taxis in Berlin decided to change their mind and reneged on the deal.

We were all more than heartbroken. We felt devastated.

Chapter Ten
Going Back

It was 1980 and twenty years since I had been free to visit the United States.

I had kept in touch with the legal position and had learned that both the Federal authorities and the State of New York had become convinced of my innocence and were prepared to drop the charges against me.

However, as I had jumped bail and, whilst it was still a misdemeanor and not a crime, there was no statute of limitation.

There was only one solution—return.

I knew that going back to America I would have to face the courts, but even worse, the resultant publicity. However, it was equally true that if I didn't take action now, I would loose my nerve and then have to spend the rest of my life unable to visit the US and blame this fact for everything I failed to achieve.

My Canadian lawyer introduced me to a wonderful New York based criminal attorney, formerly a star performer with the FBI. His experiences had been the subject of a successful and critically acclaimed movie. I felt in good hands and my Canadian lawyer and I crossed the border to the US. I will never forget how much strength and courage I got through him.

My American attorney was surprised by the number of reporters, photographers and press that showed up for my first appearance in court.

Maria was in Holland at the time pursuing her decision to become a qualified psychotherapist. On her way to breakfast Maria was totally shocked when she saw my face looking at her from the front page of all the London Sunday Papers, neatly laid out by the reception desk, for the hotel guests.

The next few weeks were agonizing, as I awaited the verdict of the courts.

Finally, my worries were over.

I was fined, as I recall, US$ 5,000 in the Federal Court and in New York State, another US$ 500.

Filled with a joy, I cannot describe—I was free again to travel to and in the US.

Maria and I celebrated with a few days of theatre going in New York and re-visiting my old haunts, which I remembered so well and had truly missed. Then we left for L.A. together and, during the flight, I told Maria that I was really nervous. I needn't have feared. I was welcomed back by old friends and associates and was quickly in touch with the current scene.

On the second day, on the way to our hotel, Maria noticed a familiar name. Celeste Yarnell, the young leading lady from *Eve*, had become one of the foremost real estate agents in Beverly Hills.

"Well," Maria remarked, "Celeste finally has her name in a box."

Fanny Hill was now completed and I screened it for Hugh Hefner at his renowned Playboy mansion. Hef and his then girlfriend loved the movie and Hef bought it on the spot.

The Playboy Channel had just recently been launched. I worked out a deal for a package of films, mainly based on Classics of Erotica with the friendly ex-NBC executive who ran the company. The films were to be produced in Europe.

I quickly wrote the scripts and embarked on the filming.

In Spain, we shot *Black Venus*, inspired by the tale by Balzac. I employed a Bahamian beauty queen, Lolita Armbrister, who was living in L.A. We became good friends and still are. I asked if Lolita wanted to change her name to Josephine Jacqueline Jones, better known as J.J., she loved it.

I found that she had a most interesting career. At the age of 18, she had been Miss Nassau, in the Bahamas, and had gone on to Miami for a beauty pageant. There allegedly, she had been introduced to Senator Edward Kennedy, of the famous Kenney family, and became his mistress and traveled with him all over the United States. (For further reference Lolita wrote a biography, *Bahamas Fever*)

Again, allegedly, Lolita heard a rumor that the Kennedy family believed her to be pregnant and wanted to, allegedly, put a contract on her life as they didn't want any black Kennedy's around. The rumor was a lot of nonsense, but she went back to the Bahamas and became the friend of the then Prime Minister, Mr. Pindling.

In that capacity she became his ambassadress to the Caribbean and traveled all over the islands. J.J. went to Haiti and had an affair with the son of "Papa Doc" and then came back to Nassau just to coincide with the visit of the Shah of Iran, who had fled from Persia after the revolution, on his way to his ultimate refuge.

At any rate, J.J. was a very nice girl, a lot of fun to be around. After reading the script, she really wanted to play the part, having no problems with nudity or sex in general.

I invited her first to Rome though we where ultimately going to make the picture in Madrid. In Rome, she gave an example of her savvy in worldly matters.

J.J. called me from the airport to say she couldn't come into the country because she didn't have a visa and with a Bahamian passport she needed one to enter the country. I got busy calling all sorts of people I knew in government to get the visa for her. Well I needn't have worried. Lolita arrived escorted from the airport by the Chief of the Airport Carrabenieri. J.J. lived like a lady and was a lady.

She made the picture for me in Madrid which was highly publicized in the local press including the English language newspaper which circulated all over Spain in those days. At that time the reputedly richest man in the world, Adnan Khashoggi was living in his villa at the Costa Brava.

Adnan adopted J.J. Through him she met most members of the Saudi Arabian Royal family and became the possessor of a remarkable collection of jewelry.

Whenever J.J. was in London, she would, with my knowledge, stay at my home when I wasn't there. At one time, a burglar burst into the apartment. It was almost impossible to prevent, short of having bars on the windows which I certainly did not want.

The burglar demanded her money or her body. J.J. said she had no money, her body was available, but she unfortunately suffered from AIDS.

The burglar fled. No doubt he informed his compatriot burglars at Wormwood Scrubs, the next time he went to jail.

There was another burglary at the apartment when J.J. wasn't there. I was away too. The burglars virtually took the place apart looking for the jewelry they didn't find; even cutting through the paintings on the walls. That hurt. Some of the paintings were of Ellen Terry, the last of my mementos of my father who knew her well and whose favorite actress she was.

In France, I was making *Frank and I* a well known Victorian novella.

For my third film, in which J.J. also appeared, I updated Arthur Schnitzler's *La Ronde* and called it *Love Circles*. The setting was contemporary and I embarked on a schedule of filming in Paris, Cannes, Hong Kong, Los Angeles and New York. For a modest budget film, this was quite a challenge, but I pulled it off and the resultant production was very well received.

I completed the package of five films with *Christina*, an original title, filmed in Majorca and another subject shot in the US. I owned the foreign rights on these films and I decided to sell them, in Cannes, during the Festival. I took five double pages in *Variety*.

Cannon, run by my friends, Menahem Golan and his cousin Yoram Globus, had some thirty pages of advertisements in the same issue. Hank Werba, the Rome correspondent of *Variety*, told me, that at the daily luncheon table, where the various journalists met, I was known as: "The one man Cannon." I laughed and replied, that I was well aimed, sometimes unfortunately, loaded, but completely impossible to fire.

I felt then, and now, that this may be a suitable epitaph.

It was also Hank Werba who wrote of me: "Harry Towers is the only man I know who can walk into any town with an empty suitcase and walk out with a movie."

Meantime, I went on to successfully sell, with some help from MGM, the *Classics of Erotica* all over world. I was later to dub the genre, Science Fuck-tion.

Back in L.A., I also developed my connection with the new cable channel operated by Disney. I discussed various projects with them and they asked me, if they could take a look at a recent work of mine, preferably a costume piece. I, rather nervously, sent them a video of *Fanny Hill*.

They liked it and were impressed.

I warned them, however, that if I was to make a period subject for the Disney Channel, I would require a somewhat larger budget.

When they asked for the reason, I explained that the wardrobe would be more costly, due to the fact that the ladies in the cast would be wearing more clothes.

I am glad to say that they saw the joke and committed themselves to a screenplay I had written, based on Robert Louis Stevenson's *Black Arrow*. I asked my old friend, John Hough, to direct and we went to Spain. Oliver Reed headed the cast, together with Donald Pleasance and the great Spanish actor, Fernando Rey. Disney was very pleased with the result.

I had become aware that the video market was growing steadily and I began an association with one of the far-seeing men who had pioneered its growth, Austin Furst, the independently thinking founder of Vestron.

When I suggested to him that we should develop an Italian classic subject, the last days of Pompeii into a modest budget exploitation movie, designed for a video release, we made a deal. The film was shot in Italy and the cast included Sybil Danning, Donald Pleasance and J.J.

My next project with Vestron was to be shot in South Africa, so I flew to Johannesburg. My arrival coincided with the proclamation of a State of Emergency by the South African Government.

I moved on to Mauritius to make the film, but I started to have problems with Vestron. When I returned to Johannesburg, I met with Avi Lerner, an Israeli business man, who represented Cannon in South Africa, together with his head of production, John Stodel.

They had recently completed two films in Zimbabwe for Cannon *King Solomon's Mines* and the sequel, based on the same subject I'd already filmed in Swaziland *Allan Quartermain* and entitled *King Solomon's Treasure*.

Avi had expressed interest in developing more subjects to put the tax shelter investments he had developed to good use. They combined a number of highly commercial elements. I had heard about a very successful Science Fiction books by John Norman, all involving a mythical country called "Gor."

I acquired the rights, and with the help of a copy of the books and a current issue of Playboy, which featured our young star Rebecca Ferratti, I signed a deal memo with Menaham Golan on a fire hydrant in New York, where he was directing a movie. I went straight on to the airport to catch my flight to South Africa.

I assembled a crew, mainly of South Africans, who I already knew well and started to build the elaborate sets we required for the two films we intended to produce "back to back."

For *Gor* the first film, I brought back another dear old friend, Oliver Reed and for the second film, *Outlaw or Gor*, two more friends, Herbert Lom and Jack Palance.

I quickly realized that the South African tax shelter law represented a wonderful opportunity to make movies in the country I already knew so well. I resolved to continue my close and friendly association with Cannon in the USA, but also develop other new opportunities.

I changed an old title *Coast of Skeletons* to *Skeleton Coast* and wrote a new script, with contemporary settings. I persuaded Ernest Borgnine to come to South Africa to star in the film along with another American actor, Robert Vaughan.

Robert was a fine man with a great reputation, but somewhat of a conservative. He arrived on a Sunday, when the best restaurant in the hotel, the Sandton Sun in Johannesburg, was closed, so I booked a table at a first class Italian restaurant in Sandton.

Oliver Reed, who was staying in the same hotel, phoned to say that he was lonely and asked if he could join us for dinner. I agreed. I should have known that this was a mistake. Olly turned up roaring drunk and insisted on showing to Robert his most prized possession, his penis with a great big eagle tattooed on it.

Oliver climbed up on the table, opposite Robert Vaughan, and opened his fly to give him a better view. When this attracted the attention of the other customers in the restaurant, Oliver lowered his pants, exposed his bum and gave the Victory Sign. I hurried a startled Robert Vaughan out of the restaurant and back to the hotel.

The following morning, I encountered Olly with a sheepish look on his face as he emerged from his hotel room. "I hope I didn't embarrass you last night," was his contribution. "You bloody well did," I replied, "don't do it again." And he never did.

It was not generally known, but Oliver Reed was in fact the illegitimate descendant of one of the great theatrical knights of the Edwardian era, Sir Herbert Beerbohm Tree.

It was Tree who first built and operated Her Majesty's Theatre in the Haymarket, and, as I have related earlier, my father started his life in the theatre in London as the box office manager for Tree at Her Majesty's Theatre.

On a later occasion, for another film, I had a slight dispute with Oliver and his younger brother, who became his personal manager, over the question of billing. I related to them an incident concerning Tree, which my father had told to me many years before.

Each year, Tree mounted elaborate productions at her Majesty's Theatre, such as *David Copperfield*, where Tree played both Mr. Micawber and Uriah Heep.

He always had a large supporting cast and each year, at the closing of the season, there was a tradition whereby he interviewed each member of his repertory company, thanked them for their work, and engaged them for the following season.

One year, the last of the company to meet him was a somewhat aged and rather pedestrian actor, who had a special request.

"Sir Herbert," he explained, "this will be my tenth season with you, and I'd like some kind of recognition. It's not just the money, but the billing.

Could my name be placed in the final position, preceded by the word 'and'?" the actor asked.

Sir Herbert gently and thoughtfully stroked his legendary beard, before replying, "How about 'but'?"

Oliver Reed's response to the story was: "Harry, I'll never talk to you about billing again."

For our next two productions in South Africa, we turned to another successful series of books, *Dragonard* and its sequel *Master of Dragonard Hill*. These were tales of an island in the Caribbean, an ex British colony, dealing with a slave revolt and concerned with the incestuous relationships between the colonists and their slaves.

For one of the leading roles, I brought to South Africa one of my favorite actresses, who I had known and admired since Orson called her "the most fascinating woman in the world": Eartha Kitt.

I knew Eartha as an outstanding black activist and I was concerned as to how she would fare in a still intensely racist state, South Africa, I need not have worried. Eartha is also a diplomat. She was a success wherever she went. Eartha became a personal friend of the wife of the bigoted Prime Minister and a guest of the government in Cape Town, where she was invited to attend every state function.

The one person who wouldn't meet with her was, Winnie Mandela, who considered she had betrayed her race by coming to South Africa. Years later, I was to meet Winny when she was a Government Minister.

I still prefer Eartha Kitt, though I've never heard Winny Mendella sing.

With the *Dragonard* films, I continued my successful relationship with Cannon. I was spending a considerable amount of time in Los Angeles, where they were riding high. They had opened a new office building in Buena Vista and with their slogan, "This is the Year of Cannon," they were seeking to conquer the world, the world of Hollywood that is.

I had known Menahem Golan and Yoram Globus from their very beginning and had always liked them. I think the feeling was mutual. I also made good friends with their principle executive, an Englishman and ex-production manager, Christopher Pearce.

Chris told me how, after meeting the cousins on a film *The Uranium Conspiracy*, they offered him a job in their then modest office in New York. When he arrived he found them in the middle of a stupendous argument, shouting and gesturing, all in Hebrew. Chris, who couldn't understand a word, crept out of their small office and consulted their Israeli secretary.

"Oh," she explained. "They are arguing as to which deli they should order their lunch from." So went matters at Cannon.

By the time I was working with them in Los Angeles, there were more important matters to argue about, but their style was the same. I had already made a small film for them on location in Hollywood, staring Mickey Rooney, entitled *White Stallion*.

Among the projects they had supported for some time was an Alistair MacLean property, *River of Death*. They had considered shooting the film in various locations, including South America, and throughout these expensive pre-production activities, (they'd invested over a million dollars), they'd kept the director, Steve Carver, on their pay roll.

I suggested to them we should make the film in South Africa, and star Michael Dudikof, who they had under contract. They agreed and I went to work. Then, on Saturday morning, Menahem arrived in the office, having completed his weekend shopping. He tossed at me a paperback he had picked up in the store. The title was *Platoon Leader*. The film *Platoon* had just opened with considerable success.

"We make it too." he declared, "back to back."

I read the book, which was written by a veteran of the war in Vietnam.

I checked that the rights were available and turned it into a working screenplay within a week, added a budget and a tentative schedule. Cannon was financed by the subsidiary of a French bank, the Credit Lyonnaise, in Holland, which enjoyed considerable autonomy.

I filled in the Application Form they required to cover the two films. I paused at the category, "Development." For *Platoon Leader*, I put down a $1.50, the cost of the paperback. The bank didn't comment on the application which was approved.

Chapter Eleven
Action and More Action

In South Africa, we decided to shoot *Platoon Leader* in the Durban area. We rented an old sugar plantation, changed the landscape to resemble Vietnam, and imported from the Durban Zoo, a single water buffalo, who appeared, shot from various angles, in practically every scene. Michael Dudikof starred in both films. We had one problem. We needed Vietnamese extras for the battle scenes. To make up the number, we could use Africans. But for the front row, clearly visible to the camera, we needed oriental faces.

That summer, it was difficult to get prompt service at any Chinese restaurant in Durban. The waiters were all "otherwise engaged."

The film was directed by Aaron Norris, the younger brother of Chuck Norris.

One night, when I was present on location, I saw him deal with a serious problem. An argument between some of the members of the cast had developed into a fight, and Aaron waded in with his fists to settle matters.

He had, I observed, "the Norris touch." It was lethal.

Working on *Platoon Leader* was Anita Hope. She was to become my personal assistant and work with me faithfully for eight years. I attended her beautiful wedding and am glad to say that she is still happily married with a family, living in Los Angeles.

For *River of Death*, we moved down the coast from Durban, to Port Saint John, a little known trading settlement in a remote area. It made a perfect location for this story, set in South America. I spent a considerable amount of time during this production commuting between the bank in Rotterdam and Cannon in Los Angeles, to ensure that the money kept flowing down the river to Port Saint John.

Our supporting cast featured the usual suspects, including Herbert Lom, Donald Pleasence and happily, Robert Vaughan. The flow of pictures with which we provided Cannon were all successful, and helped to support some of the other, and more expensive, productions in which they were engaged.

Meantime, I completed two other films in South Africa for other companies, one of the *Howling* series and a remake, loosely based on my big commercial success, *99 Women*.

Although substantially occupied working in South Africa, I maintained my regular habit of being in Cannes for the Film Festival.

Cannon had reached the peak of its success by acquiring the EMI group. The acquisition occurred just before Cannes and Cannon plastered all the poster sites which advertised the EMI pictures with a large slip, identifying them as "A CANNON FILM."

My friend Walter Manley observed that he had seen nothing like it in his entire life in show business.

As this chapter is rather short, I'm taking the opportunity to reminisce about an occasion when I heard a radio interview with the famous and brilliant director, Billy Wilder.

The interviewer asked Wilder what his inspiration was for his "masterpiece" *The Apartment* that he co-wrote and directed. Billy Wilder replied that he was motivated by seeing Noël Coward's *Brief Encounter* that led him to ask himself "where they did it."

In 1960 and 1961, during the most troubled and tragic period of my life to date, I happened to see *The Apartment* three times. The first time was at its premiere at Radio City Music Hall in N.Y. The second time, I saw it in a cinema on the Champs Elyseés, in Paris, which was also the first night I spent with Mariella Novotny and the third time was in Budapest, Hungary, where, to my surprise, I had discovered a subtitled version playing in a small cinema. I have since then seen the film on TV a number of times with Maria, much happier times I am glad to say. It's a wonderful film. It always makes me want to cry—with laughter.

I heard on the BBC, today, a report from Katmandu, capital of Nepal.

The report was on the improving political situation. It failed, however, to mention the biggest problem in Nepal—the rapid and continuing decline in the population.

You see—"Katmandu"—but "Kat-women–don't."

Here's an older story:
A man with a hearing impediment endeavors to buy a Postal Order. The Post Office attendant examines his application written in pencil. "I'm sorry, sir, but I'm afraid you'll have to ink it over"

The man is absent for half an hour of consideration, before he returns to the Post Office attendant, to whom he explains, "I've thought it over, and I still want to buy the Postal Order."

Just one more for the road:
A man from the Far East approaches the Bureau de Change at London's Victoria Station. He changes some money. Dissatisfied with the result of the exchange, the man complains, "How come, every time I change the same amount of money, I keep getting less in return?

The clerk at the Bureau de Change explains, with sorrow, "Fluctuations, fluctuations, sir"

The foreigner responds: "And fluck you British, too."

In 1990 I was in Los Angeles and managed to find and hire two famous and exceptional artists, Burgess Meredith and Don Ameche.

I persuaded them to commit themselves to co-star in a film I was about to produce in Malawi, South Africa, called *Odd Ball Hall*. Their performances were memorable. The film, I regret to say was not. Alas, all too often the same applies to life itself.

Heigh Ho, Heigh Ho…

Chapter Twelve
Films Come in Cannes

I'll digress for a moment with my favorite Cannes story.

An attractive French starlet, on her first visit to Cannes, is being interviewed on the beach by Tele Monte Carlo. Asked to name the men that she has met with whom she would like to have an affair, she names two contemporary and popular American stars at the time Richard Gere and Bruce Willis. Pressed for a third entry, she comes up with the name of a particularly obnoxious American producer.

"Purquoi, Monsieur…?" enquires the interviewer

"Ah," replies the starlet, "I go to all the parties and receptions and I always hear the same advice. "Fuck Monsieur….."

I interrupted my work in South Africa to make another film.

I had commissioned a talented Canadian writer, Ron Raley, to write a screenplay, based upon my idea to combine the familiar story by Robert Louis Stevenson, *Dr. Jekyll and Mr. Hyde*, with some of the elements of the Jack the Ripper Case. Anthony Perkins liked the script and agreed to accept the leading role.

To establish the atmosphere of Victorian England, which was essential to the atmosphere of our story, we began filming near the South Side of Clapham Common, a few streets from where I had lived as a boy. The main shooting, however, was in Budapest, another city I knew quite well. The film was successfully released under the title of *Edge of Sanity*

I returned to South Africa to produce yet another version of Agatha Christies' *Ten Little Indians*, this time with the alternative title of *Death on a Safari*. Donald Pleasence portrayed the murderous judge.

I also produced another Michael Dudikoff film in the *American Ninja* series. But the "good days" at Cannon were drawing to a close.

The acquisition of EMI had been followed by a suspension of trading in their shares on the New York Stock Exchange. They were in trouble and sought help wherever they hoped it might be available. Through their bankers they met an Italian entrepreneur, Giancarlo

Perretti, who was reputed to have a strong Mafia connection. In their large and still imposing premises at Cannes, during the Festival, I noticed a number of strangers in dark glasses.

Chris Pearce alerted me to the fact that under the new management, I must anticipate the frequent presence of auditors. I responded that I was not so much concerned with the presence of "Price Waterhouse," but that I was distinctly alarmed, in the words of George Raft, at the sight of any "Smith and Wesson."

Despite the alarming situation, I still had faith that the friendship and resource of Menaham and Yoram would ensure their survival.

Menahem was In Budapest engaged on directing a new version of *The Beggars Opera*, under the title of *Mack the Knife*. I visited him in Hungary and we discussed remaking *The Phantom of the Opera*, which Menahem mistakenly believed, was in the public domain. I had the idea of starring in the remake, Robert Englund, now successfully identified as Freddy in the big hit, *Nightmare on Elm Street*, the project which had launched New Line into the big time.

When I approached him, Robert Englund liked the idea and agreed to make the movie. We'd already agreed to shoot the film in Budapest and utilize and adapt some of the big sets built for Menahem's film. Filming was soon under way in Hungary. But we had another problem.

Encouraged by Perretti, Yoram and Menahem had decided to part company. I was devastated. I liked them both but in different ways. There was a saying that the difference between them was that Yoram knew the budget and Menahem knew the story. However, the breakup left me in an embarrassing position. I didn't know whom to turn to, to ensure that we could meet the payroll and complete the movie. It was Menahem who took over the project.

He was determined to make a good film and spared no expense. After some sneak previews, we shot additional scenes both in Los Angeles and New York. Menahem had organized a major release and, in anticipation of a success, I'd already written and had prepared a sequel film *The Phantom of Manhattan*.

On the Saturday morning, following its Friday premiere in the States, we sat around in Menahem's office in Los Angeles and heard the sad news. It was not a hit.

Despite our other problems, I'd continued to make films in South Africa and had embarked on a program of horror movies based on the Edgar Allan Poe stories, *Buried Alive*, *The Fall of the House of Usher*, and *The Masque of the Red Death*. We somehow overcame our difficulties and completed all three films.

I had also managed to retain my friendship with Menahem and his new company Twenty First Century, and with Yoram, where Cannon had merged with MGM. But this deal was coming apart, and Menahem, too, with his incurable but wonderful optimism, had troubles ahead.

Yet, I had to keep working, and another old friend, the imaginative banker, Lew Horwitz, came to my help. Lew, who had been a director of Cannon, was famous for a series of illustrated advertisements in the trade press. I only once earned his displeasure, when I told him, as a joke, that a group of his friends were planning to salute him with a full page ad in *Variety*.

For the art work, they had visualized a full page reproduction of the armless Venus de Milo, with the caption: "Thank you, Lew Horwitz." Lew was not amused.

In a friendlier mood, Lew now introduced me to Frank Agrama, a highly successful distributor and property magnate, with an impressive office on Sunset Boulevard.

Frank was developing a contact with the government in Luxembourg, who had launched a unique tax shelter scheme. Frank needed a project and I had one in mind.

I'd long cherished the idea of returning to the works of Sir Arthur Conan Doyle and seeking fresh inspiration from the adventures of Sherlock Holmes. I came up with the title, *The Golden Years of Sherlock Holmes.*

Frank liked the idea, but his advisers wanted the project in the form of a mini series. Instinct advised me that this was not such a good idea.

The essence of Holmes was brevity, and Doyle's best work had been in the form of the short story. I felt that four hours of airtime to tell a Sherlock Holmes adventure would be too long. However I came up with first story line.

I visualized Holmes in Vienna to attend the first night of Franz Lehar's *The Merry Widow* and we went to work on the script.

For the roles of Holmes and Dr. Watson, we obtained the services of Christopher Lee and Patrick Macnee, which was excellent casting. We found all the locations we needed among the streets and squares of Luxembourg Ville, and the castles of the little principality. We had one difficulty; we could not clear the rights to *The Merry Widow* and substituted *Die Fledermaus.* We had a line in the script, which got lost on the cutting room floor, where Watson questioned Holmes about the change.

"Elementary, my dear Watson," Holmes responded. "It's public domain."

We continued shooting the miniseries, but for some reason. Frank Agrama was getting worried. Shooting in Luxembourg was expensive. Both technicians and cast had to be imported, fed and housed. Prince Alessandro Tasca, whom I had known years ago when he was with the Completion Guarantors in Rome, was in charge of production. Despite all his experience, he was still an optimist.

"Give me," he used to say, "a city with a bankrupt treasury and fighting in the streets and you'll find it's a good place to make a movie. They'll be so grateful you bothered to come."

We had a strange cocktail of nationalities. To save money, Tasca had brought many of the crew from Yugoslavia. The director was Hungarian, and the camera crew were from London together with some of the departmental heads. The catering, which was appalling, apart from the special meals served at Tasca's table, was Italian. By the end of the shooting, the relationships between the nationalities were so bad that each had a separate wrap party. I chose the safest route and took the entire Luxembourg crew, all three drivers, two of them immigrants from other European countries, to dinner.

To salvage the losses in Luxembourg, I recommended to Frank Agrama that we shoot the second Sherlock Holmes miniseries he planned to make, in Zimbabwe, where I knew from experience that costs would be more reasonable and easy to control. As for the subject for the Holmes adventure, I already had an idea.

Some years earlier, when setting up the remake of *Ten Little Indians* that we later shot in South Africa, I had paid a visit to the Victoria Falls, as a possible location. There was a tradition with visitors to take the "booze cruise" at sunset, which stopped briefly at an island on the Zambezi River, upstream from the falls. I heard that it was known as Kandahar Island.

I knew vaguely that Kandahar was a provincial town in Afghanistan, but I failed to see the connection. Then I remembered, Lord Roberts of Kandahar, who was ennobled for his leadership in the Second Afghan War and lived on until the first World War, to inspire the British Empire as "Bobs" Roberts. He must clearly have at one time, visited the Falls.

This set my mind to the thought of what other internationally famous personalities might have visited the area at the turn of the century. I came up with the names of President Theodore Roosevelt and Lilly Langtry, mistress of King Edward VII.

I only had to add Sherlock Holmes and Dr. Watson to the mix and I had found the idea for *The Incident At Victoria Falls* and the story line for the second miniseries in *The Golden Years of Sherlock Holmes*.

With a largely South African crew and the help of the Zimbabwe authorities we restored the Victoria Falls Hotel to its original condition and played host to the cast and crew. For this one special occasion the Zimbabwe Government permitted the Union Jack to fly again and, as an aging Richard Todd as "Bob" Roberts, rode up with his escort of Imperial Cavalry, to greet Sherlock Holmes, I realized that, once again, I had made my dreams come true.

I persuaded Frank Agrama to sponsor another production in Zimbabwe, based on the successful results of our first expedition.

I turned once more to Sir Arthur Conan Dole for inspiration. I wrote a screenplay based on his work, *The Lost World*. Then, I provided a sequel, *Return to the Lost World*. I shot both films in Zimbabwe as Canadian/South African co-productions, though the treaty between the two countries had yet to be signed.

For the role for Professor Challenger, I cast John Rhys-Davies, and for his critical and sardonic partner, David Warner. From Canada I brought Timothy Bond to direct and Eric McCormack to star as Edward Malone.

Although it was of no help to us, the subject was to attract other versions of the same story, including a remake in Quebec, starring Patrick Bergin, and a long running On Hour Series, produced in Australia. I have recently learned that yet another high budget television remake is in the works.

If imitation is the sincerest form of flattery, we have certainly been flattered.

I had kept in touch with Anthony Perkins, an actor I liked and admired a lot. I had commissioned a script based on a classic subject, *The Mummy*.

Anthony Perkins liked the idea and approved the script. Yoram Globus had, as I mentioned, parted company with Cannon, but approved the project, provided it was shot in Israel, where he owned a studio.

I learned that his financing deal would cover two films and I suggested we shoot both films back to back. When I arrived in Israel, I found that Tobe Hooper had been hired to direct the second film, whilst Gerry O'Hara, who I had under contract, would direct *The Mummy*. But we had another problem.

Anthony Perkins was sick, and would within a month, tragically die of AIDS.

We finally engaged Tony Curtis, who I had never met to replace him. Tobe Hooper, who I learned to like very much, had his own ideas for the second film that was later released as *Tobe Hooper's Nightmare*.

This was my first experience of shooting in Israel and I enjoyed it.

Most of our work was in and around Tel Aviv, but we visited Jerusalem and shot in the famous American Colony Hotel, itself an inspiration for a movie I still hope to make *Jerusalem Cop*, with Topol of *Fiddler on the Roof* fame, in the title role. The two films I had made with Yoram Globus were safely completed and I was looking for fresh fields to conquer. I knew that Tobe Hooper had a long relationship with the writer, Stephen King.

I knew that my English partner on my earlier film with Anthony Perkins, *Edge of Sanity*, had just released a Stephen King subject *The Lawnmower Man* and was being sued by Stephen King, who objected to the credits who referred to this earlier work as "a Stephen King" film.

I was aware that my partner, Ed Simons, owned another early work of Stephen King, *The Mangler*, and that whilst he was involved in litigation with Stephen King, it would be difficult to launch.

I had another associate, Anant Singh, who was anxious to make films in South Africa, and was potentially very interested in a Stephen King project. Anant and I became good friends and have remained thus through all the years since, which is rather rare in this business

Anant bought the rights to *The Mangler* from Ed, and I co-wrote with Tobe Hooper a new screenplay. I had little difficultly in persuading Robert Englund to play the lead and we made the film in Johannesburg.

I owned another property which Anant was interested in acquiring, the remake rights in Alan Paton's *Cry the Beloved Country*. I had met the author years before and knew of his disappointment with the Korda version, with a young Sidney Poitier, for which, incidentally, he hadn't earned a penny.

I went to work with Anant to commission a screenplay from Ronald Harwood, South African born, and best known for his most enjoyable play and film *The Dresser*. Ronald told me he would want a higher fee than for the previous occasion on which he had worked for me. I could not recall the previous occasion, but Ronald proceeded to remind me that, when I was running ATV, I had produced a version of Charles Dickens *Bardell Versus Pickwick* starring a famous British actor, Sir Donald Wolfit. "I was his dresser," explained Ronald.

I introduced Anant to James Earl Jones, who agreed to star in *Cry the Beloved Country*. Anant made the film in South Africa, where in due course, Richard Harris joined the cast.

I had known Anant for many years, since he bought the South African Rights for *Fanny Hill*. I must say, that Anant, a good friend of Nelson Mandela, is one of the most socially conscious, creative, humanitarian and reliable people in show business, which makes him a wonderful exception. I am very proud to be able to call Anant my friend.

After the very successful premiere in New York which Hilary Clinton attended, I moved on.

I visited Israel where I was accompanied Lew Horwitz, my banker who did business there. One morning Lew telephoned my room and invited me to join him in visiting a bank. I dressed accordingly and met him downstairs, where a car awaited us, driven by a stranger wearing plain clothes. We drove north from Tel Aviv and headed left into the mountains.

It was then I realized that the bank was the West Bank.

The stranger was in fact an experienced Israeli Secret Agent, whose job was to acquire land-sites from the Mayors of Palestine communities, which could then become new Israeli settlements.

There had already been several attempts on his life and his well known car was hardly the best vehicle for such a dangerous journey. We ended our trip in Jerusalem where we had rooms booked at the American Colony Hotel, a famous historic building where previous guests had included Lawrence of Arabia and Winston Churchill.

After dinner, I had a date in my room with a beautiful young lady from an Escort Agency. Thus my adventure had ended successfully. I started preparing my next venture. I had my eye on Russia.

Chapter Thirteen
My Eyes Are Red

I had last been in Russia during very difficult times, but I revisited both Moscow and Saint Petersburg to take another more recent look and to establish new contacts. What I needed was a subject with memories of the Cold War, but relevant to contemporary problems. I recalled Len Deigton's creation, Harry Palmer, the subject of three successful movies, *The Ipcress File* and two sequels.

I was familiar with Len Deighton. Some years earlier, I had bought and paid for his book, *SSGB* with a rather expensive option which cost me US $ 100,000. Despite commissioning a very good script, we couldn't get the project off the ground.

I approached Len for the right for me to write a contemporary Harry Palmer adventure. He agreed, provided Michael Caine would play the part. I made a deal with Michael to make not just one film but two.

I still had a problem, for Len Deighton didn't even have a clear title to the name, Harry Palmer. In the original book, the hero has no name. But for the film, a name was invented by the producer, Harry Saltzman.

I tracked Harry down, who was living in Paris and, after some difficult negotiations with his wife, I secured his rights.

Meantime, I'd already written the first script, ultimately entitled *Bullet To Beijing* and had a treatment ready for the second: *Midnight in Saint Petersburg.*

Now, all I needed was the money to make the movies. I'd sent the script to Matthew Duda, then and now Head of Acquisitions at the Showtime Network. Showtime agreed to put up half of the US $ 12,000,000 budget for the two movies. I planned to make them as U.K./Canadian/Russian co-productions and I was trail blazing all the way. Nobody before had even attempted such a complex international co-production, and it was a miracle that we ultimately succeeded.

I left for St. Petersburg to commence production. I was joined there, by a very bright and very young English girl, as my assistant. Her name was Juliette Benson, but I gave her the nickname, "Whippet," as she was good to look at and fast on her feet.

After completing the films in St. Petersburg, Juliette joined me in Hungary for a reconnaissance with Bob Guccione for the movie *Catherine the Great* that we planned to make together. From there, the Whippet and I went to Milan for the MIFED trade fair.

Next we were off to the Cannes Film Festival, where we screened the first of the completed "Harry Palmer" films. Thereafter we went to N.Y together and on to L.A, Hong Kong, back to the US and finally again to the Cannes Festival. It was there and then that Juliette met the man, who was to become her husband. I am glad to say that the two of them are still happily married and working for the Nielsen Company in L.A. We frequently talk on the phone and get together whenever I'm in L.A discussing the tastes of the contemporary audiences.

Russia welcomed us with open palms, awaiting a tip. My first move was to buy the protection of the Mafia and unlike some of my other new found friends, they never let me down.

The production was quite elaborate, and we had to create a scene in a London square and the Beijing railway terminal. Most of the shooting was in and about Saint Petersburg, and included the use of the Royal Palaces, the State Circus and theatre and the construction of elaborate sets at the studio of Lenfilms.

We also needed the use of a train for a week, whilst we shunted it around Saint Petersburg. The railway authorities provided the train, with an unexpected addition, there were one hundred people living onboard.

Whether or not we needed them as extras, they all expected to be fed.

When Queen Elizabeth came to Saint Petersburg, the first ever visit of a reigning British sovereign, I was invited to the official reception, held at the Youssoupoff Palace, site of the murder of Rasputin. I recognized at the entrance, representatives of both the KGB and MI5—quite a combination.

It was on the day of my 74th birthday and I was wearing my RAF tie, which was noticed by the Air Commodore of the Royal Flight. He questioned me as to what I had done whilst in the service, and when I told him that I had created *Much Binding in the March*, he treated me with the greatest respect, as though I wore the Victoria Cross. It was my birthday and I felt very happy.

When the Queen asked me what it was like to make films in Russia, I responded that it was rather like remaking *Jurassic Park* but with one big difference, real live dinosaurs.

I had brought from Canada the Hungarian born George Mihalka. He did quite a good job, but every day he came to me with a different problem. Our schedule and or financing were based on completing two films in twelve weeks. We were in our ninth week of Principal Photography and we hadn't even started shooting the second movie. Then, George fell off a ladder. Despite his injuries, George bravely completed the scenes for his first film.

The second film *Midnight in St.Petersburg* was directed by another very competent Canadian director, Douglas Jackson. As we neared completion, we had another panic.

A journalist from the London Daily Mail wrote a piece about the filming, headlined "Why The Russian Mafia is out to get Michael Caine." Michael was terrified and wanted to leave Russia immediately. A stern message from the Completion Guarantors and the diplomacy of Michael's beautiful wife, Shakira, convinced him to stay for a week and complete both films.

I had been anxious that we depart from Russia without any problems and I had overestimated our cash requirements. Our last problem was to export the surplus cash. The solution—Western Union.

When I was making the two pictures in St. Petersburg with Michael Caine, I had the idea of doing a film about Rasputin. HBO did such a film and they asked my advice about shooting in Russia. They told me they were taking a Hungarian crew with them to Russia and I said, "I don't know what your experience will be, but I will bet even money that you will end up making the film in Budapest," which is exactly what happened.

I had the idea of doing Rasputin in rather a different fashion. First of all I was going to get Roman Polanski involved as director and bring in his usual writer and for the role of Rasputin I wanted Jack Nicholson; so while I was in St. Petersburg, I arranged to fly to Paris to take Roman, who I knew quite well, to lunch at Fouquet's.

I explained the whole plan to him and how exciting it would be under his direction, with Jack Nicholson and his wonderful look, playing Rasputin. Polanski asked me for a few details of Rasputin's life.

Finally, I asked, "Well, are you interested in moving forward?"

He said, "I'm afraid not. Now that I know more about Rasputin I have an objection to being involved with a picture about the gentleman."

I asked for the reason and he said: "Too biographical." I always thought that was a great retort and I have never forgotten it.

After my experiences in Russia, I decided to take it easy for a while. I invited Bob Guccione, the owner of Penthouse Magazine, to join me, whilst we were shooting in Russia. I'd met Bob previously, through Austin Furst of Vestron.

Austin had given a script I had written to Bob, based on the erotic classic *Moll Flanders*. Bob had already produced and, partly directed, one movie, the notorious *Caligula*. He'd always wanted to make another one and he liked *Moll Flanders*. I suggested Ken Russell as a director and Bob brought him to New York, where they met. Matters progressed and Ken rewrote, and, in my opinion, greatly improved the script.

We'd even progressed to casting the leading lady, a nubile young English model, approved by Bob. But troubles lay ahead for I saw that Bob and Ken had very different visions of what constituted an erotic movie. I left the scene, amicably. The movie was never made and Bob and Ken ended up suing each other.

Here is the reason I had invited Bob to Russia, I knew that one of his ambitions had always been to make a film about Catherine the Great. I took Bob to visit the possible historic locations and he asked me to work with him to develop the script and set up the production. I agreed, willingly, as I liked both the project and Bob personally.

Bob abandoned the idea of shooting the film in Russia, as he feared a kidnap and ransom experience. I suggested as an alternative, Budapest. We went to Hungary and progressed as far as hiring a brilliant Italian Art Director, whose set designs were approved by Bob. We needed a star for the role of the mature Catherine, and Faye Dunaway read the script, which was now complete, met with Bob and agreed to play the part. But still, the movie didn't get made.

My business has always been to make movies, not talk about making movies, however handsomely I get paid. I stayed friends with Bob, which I still am, but moved on.

I'd heard about a tax shelter agreement in a place close to my London home, but which I'd never visited, the Isle of Man. I went there and found a lot of money and a lot of sheep. How could I combine these two attractions and make a movie?

As usual, I had an idea.

I remembered, from prewar, a successful film which starred the famous Scots comedian, Will Fyffe, Margaret Lockwood and a lovable sheepdog. The movie was called *Owd Bob*.

Again, I will digress for a moment.

I'd met Will Fyffe during the War, in Glasgow, where I was staging a gala broadcast.

Will took me out, first to a pub, for a dram of "the good stuff," illegally brewed pure malt whisky, and then, to his local newsagents. I noted that Will only bought the newspapers and periodicals handed to him by the proprietor. He only purchased those which mentioned his name.

Will had his own canny and economic way of operating his personal Press Cutting Service. I can still hear Will in my mind leading an audience in singing the famous song he wrote. Will, when singing the song, always appeared to be intoxicated, but he was never drunk:

"I belong to Glasgow, Good old Glasgow town, But there's something the matter with Glasgow, It's going round and round, I'm only a poor old working man, As anyone here, can see, But after a couple of drinks on a Saturday, Glasgow belongs to me."

And whilst Will lived, it did.

Apart from perpetuating the Scots tradition for being mean, Will Fyffe was associated in the profession, with another and more valued quality, loyalty. Will first entered the big time world of vaudeville when he topped the bill at the legendary music hall, the Argyle, in Birkenhead, and received the then princely salary of one hundred pounds a week. His agent then and until the day he died; was one Tom Pacey, also from Glasgow.

Tom Pacey acknowledged this loyalty every week in a small box ad which always graced the front page of the trade periodical *The Performer*.

What neither the readers nor the profession knew was that whether Will Fyffe starred in a Hollywood movie or topped the bill at the London Palladium, Tom Pacey always received the same compensation—Just ten pounds.

This reminds me of two other tales concerning another important profession, the agent.

Gracie Fields, and also Stanley Holloway, had a similar but more generous attitude toward their agents, Bert Aza and his brother, who changed his name to Archie Pitt, with whom they remained for the whole of their professional lives.

It was Archie who originally discovered Gracie Fields, who, although having been a child actress at her local theatre, worked at the saw mill in Rochester. Archie promised to make her a star and toured her throughout the provinces in a revue entitled, incidentally "Mr. Towers of London" which made it to the West End. Later on the two of them got married.

In the days of telegraphic addresses, Bert Aza's was, memorably for an agent, Unpitied London.

A final story, this time about the legendary, Al Parker, agent for, among other stars, James Mason. Al was an irascible American, who had originally come to London to direct quota quickies. He had a foul temper and a capacity for hate.

At one time, he transposed the traditional attitude of talent to their agents, and memorably proclaimed, referring to the artists "I don't know what the bastards do for their ninety per cent."

However the best story I know about agents or actor managers concerns Colonel Parker who controlled the career of Elvis Presley.

One time Colonel Parker was pursued by an entrepreneur who wanted the services ofElvis for one week in Australia. He finally offered the Colonel one million dollars. Colonel Parker showed interest but asked a very important question, "Well, but what's in it for ma boy?"

Enough of agents.

I had one other association with *Owd Bob* and the classic English novel on which it was based. Mickey Rooney had confided in me once that his ambition was to remake it. I worked out a deal with the Isle of Man Film Commission to make *Owd Bob* on the Island as the first U.K./Canadian co-production to take advantage of the opportunities they offered.

I brought an Anglo Canadian crew and cast to the Island and a Canadian director, Rodney Gibbons. Mickey Rooney was ready to play the male lead, but my partners preferred a younger star, which may have been a mistake. The part, instead, was portrayed by James Cromwell, already closely associated with sheep, for he played the shepherd in *Babe*. I co-wrote the screenplay.

I had known for some time that Jack Palance had always wanted to play Long John Silver in *Treasure Island*. Jack was already working with me in another movie, *Marco Polo*, and designed to take every advantage of the scenery and unique architecture available.

I'd provided suitable roles for Jack Palance, Olive Reed and others.

Jack, I knew, was of Ukrainian origin, and I thought it might be fun to invite him back to the land of his ancestors. Jack agreed.

We completed the film successfully and in the press conference that followed, in Kiev, Jack astounded the local journalist, by responding to their questions in fluent Ukrainian. Jack returned via Cannes, where we were able to announce that he could finally achieve his ambition and play Long John Silver.

Initially, I found it difficult to convince my partners that it would be possible to shoot *Treasure Island* in the British Isles, since the story is supposed to take place on an isolated island in the tropics. But I had located on the Isle of Man an area known as Island's Eye, which had the desolate and deserted appearance we were seeking.

All we needed now was a ship which we located, successfully, in Plymouth.

The director, Peter Rowe, came up with a brand new interpretation of Stevenson's timeless tale. With both, the Canadian and the U.K. subsidies and tax shelters available, plus the help of the Isle of Man Film Commission and Lew Horwitz, the money was available. The film was completed successfully.

The Canadian Government has co-production treaties with over forty different countries, and I was fascinated to learn that one of the newest to sign such a treaty was Fidel Castro's, Cuba.

The temptation was irresistible. I had to find a subject to make in Cuba. I wrote a script about contemporary Havana, using a title, I recalled, from the past *City of Fear*. This was a big mistake. A film set in contemporary Cuba was not going to work. It brought me face to face with political realities. I'd have to think again.

I'd heard that Bulgaria, which I'd visited years previously during the Communist era, was now very reasonable and interested in attracting overseas producers. I promptly changed the location and shot *City of Fear* in Sofia, with British born action star, Gary Daniels and South African born director Mark Roper. Mark directed a number of other films for me as I found him to be one of the most hands on, no nonsense, hard working, creative problem solver I know.

Next came another Zimbabwe shoot. Inspired by the land mine crisis, *High Explosive* starred Patrick Bergin.

My experience in Bulgaria had been pleasant. As yet there was no Canadian/Bulgarian co-production treaty in existence, but I went to work to rectify that fact. I lined up a program of four pictures which I went ahead and produced in Bulgaria as Canadian/U.K./Bulgarian and in two cases, Italian co-productions.

The first was *Queen's Messenger*, a contemporary action adventure, with Gary Daniels as a diplomatic courier and, John Standing as his boss, the Foreign Secretary. Next, I located, in storage, the royal train of the last King of Bulgaria. I converted it into the Orient Express and concocted a story. A terrorist invites some of the richest and most powerful folk in the world to a New Year's Eve party.

I gave it the title *Death Deceit & Destiny Aboard the Orient Express* and assembled an international cast, headed by Richard Grieco. For the third film, I turned, again, to Rider Haggard, for inspiration. My hero was the grandson of Allan Quartermain, still an explorer, portrayed by Thomas Griffith. In *High Adventure*, Quartermain goes in search of the treasure of Alexander the Great.

For my next film in Bulgaria, I finally remade Rider Haggard's *She* with a French star, Ophelia Winter, in the title role, and an excellent supporting cast, including Ian Duncan and Edward Hardwick.

The same year I completed three other films. First a new version of *Dorian* set in contemporary New York, but actually shot in Montreal, starring Malcolm McDowell in the role of Henry Wooton. What an excellent actor, as well as a warm, insightful and charming person. Happy to know him. The film turned out great and is very different from my earlier version.

Then I made a modern version of Jack London's *The Sea Wolf* in Cuba also starring, Thomas Ian Griffith and released under the title *The Pirate's Curse*.

Now is the time for me to pay tribute to my good friend, Gary Howsam. He was my co-production partner on the two films I made in the Isle of Man, five of the films I made in Bulgaria and the single film we bravely co-produced in Cuba.

Gary now heads the company, Peace Arch, quoted on the New York Stock Exchange, with branches in London and Los Angeles, very well represented in Cannes and the American Film Market. It is still a Canadian Company with its headquarters in Toronto, Canada. With the recent acquisition of a substantial library of quality films, it has become a truly international production and distribution entity. Gary Howsam makes me feel proud that in addition to my British Passport, I am also a citizen of Canada.

As you must have noticed by now, the names of famous authors have considerable attraction to me, particularly when they're in the public domain. But I've also had the privilege of working and meeting with those who were still in the land of the living. They included J.B. Priestley, Graham Greene, Ian Fleming, Leslie Charteris, Agatha Christie, Eric Ambler and several more.

The list of those who I failed to meet, alive or dead, is undoubtedly headed by Oscar Wilde. To those who had the privilege of an actual conversation with the finest wit of his time, I can only express the greatest of envy.

Another author who fascinates me is Edgar Wallace. He died in 1932, but I've enjoyed the pleasure of making films based on a number of his books. He must have been a fascinating man and I've often considered the possibility of making a film about his life. He was born in London and went to South Africa as a soldier, during the Boer War. There he tried to emulate his hero, Rudyard Kipling, who he actually met. He wrote poems and short stories about life in the army. Then he became a reporter for a news agency. But, initially through an error, copies of his despatches went directly to the London Daily Mail, who published them and gave him credit. Then he went back to London.

There his book of poems and short stories was published, but was not a success. It was accused of being too derivative of Kipling. But he did receive a welcome from the Daily Mail and its iconic owner, Lord Northcliffe. He was appointed the exclusive South African Correspondent of the Daily Mail and returned to South Africa.

There he artfully obtained the first news of the ultimate peace between the Britons and the Boers. Back in London, he started to write and ultimately achieved international success. He was very prolific, and the "Edgar Wallace Thriller of the Month" soon became an institution.

He also wrote plays—similarly prolific. As his income grew, so did his expensive style of living. He owned race horses and hoped to win the Derby. He was living beyond his means, and always short of money. But he was very resourceful. He rented a theatre in London's West End to stage one of his plays. It opened to dismal reviews; it was a disastrous flop.

But Wallace kept the theatre dark for five weeks, to enable him to write, cast, rehearse and open another play. It was a success. On another occasion, broke as usual, Wallace sent a cable to the *Chicago Tribune*, previously a good customer for newspaper serial rights, with a storyline and a request for a substantial advance on delivery of the completed work.

When the *Chicago Tribune* cabled their acceptance of his offer, Wallace dictated the novel over the weekend. The newspaper wired the money back. Wallace survived.

Near the end of his life, Wallace received an offer to go to Hollywood as a writer. There, his output included the co-authorship of the screenplay for the original *King Kong*. I was pleased to observe that the recent remake of *King Kong* honoured its obligations to the co-author. Then, Wallace, as a result of an assignation outside his bungalow at the Beverly Hills Hotel, caught a cold and died of pneumonia. He was brought back to England in state, like royalty. His epitaph is a bronze tablet secured to the wall in Ludgate Circus. The tablet is headed by his famous effigy, like that of Alfred Hitchcock which adorned the cover of all his monthly thrillers. Then follow the words, as I remember them:

Edgar Wallace
Reporter
Born London 1875
Died Los Angeles 1932
Founder member of the
Compay of Newspaper Makers.

He knew wealth and poverty, yet had
Walked with Kings and kept his bearing
Of his talents he gave lavishly to authorship
But to Fleet Street he gave his heart

I believe this is the spot where he used to sell newspapers for the *Daily Mail* when he was a boy.

The other evening, I found myself watching the original Edgar Wallace version of *King Kong* produced in 1933.

As a writer myself, I started wondering about Edgar Wallace's inspiration, when the thought occurred to me that Sir Arthur Conan Doyle's *The Lost World* had been published some years before. Now how could Conan Doyle have come up with his idea? I had the answer.

Charles Darwin's *Origin of the Species.*

It certainly pays off as a writer to see the connectedness of all things. I must say it took me a long time to realize that and to learn that there are twenty five more letters in the alphabet that the letter "I."

Without all the other letters "I" doesn't really mean anything.

In Johannesburg and Sun City, I produced a sequel to *Queen's Messenger* again with Gary Daniels and John Standing, which, to avoid confusion, was released under the title *Diamond Cut Diamond.*

It was a busy year.

The following year I completed another version of Sumuru, set in the future, starring Alexandra Kamp and directed by Darrell Roodt.

Of the producers I have admired most, Sam Spiegel is on the top of the list. I first became aware of his talents when he co-produced, under the name of S.P. Eagle *Tales From Manhattan* with an all star cast directed by Julien Duvivier.

As Sam Spiegel his credits as a producer include David Lean's *Laurence of Arabia*, *The Bridge on the River Kwai* and *On the Waterfront* as well as *The African Queen.* Sam remained active as a producer until 1983. He died two years later at the age of 84.

I cannot hope to equal his achievements, but at least I can aspire to beat his longevity as a producer. To copy the response reputably first given by Cary Grant. "How old Harry Alan Towers?"

"Old Harry Alan Towers fine, how are you?"

We're all aboard a ship of dreams—not a port in sight.

"Alright, I'll have a sherry—make it a Harvey's Bristol Cream."

Chapter Fourteen
Movies I Haven't Made
– Yet

Many people have remarked, "With all the movies you have made, you should write a book."
My response has often been: "With all the movies I haven't made, it might be a better book."

Early in my life as a film producer, I came up with an idea for a comedy to take place during a Pop Music Festival in Monte Carlo. It would concern a bank robbery, conducted by a trio of aging scoundrels, masquerading as a young pop group. First, I had the title: *The Bank Which Broke The Men From Monte Carlo*."

For the American audience we had an alternate title, *Pop Goes The World*.

The bank was a phony, the "Home and Colonial" and for the manager we cast Terry Thomas. The star was Petula Clark, an old friend and, at the time, a big name, particularly in France.

Lionel Jeffries was a Scotland Yard inspector on so frugal an expense account that he had to communicate with his superiors by way of post cards, usually dirty. Other characters included an ex Blue Bell Girl, living in luxury, in her villa at the Cap d' Antibes.

For the three old lags, I made deals with Buster Keaton, then still alive, Stanley Holloway and Groucho Marx.

Groucho was then living in a flat in Mayfair and when I went to visit him, I carried with me, as usual, a bulky briefcase. He greeted me in his usual aggressive fashion. "You're either an abortionist or a con man and, in either case, I don't trust you."

Michael Winner was the director.

The production team was hard at work in my flat in Hallam Street, when I made the alarming discovery that, in those days, to qualify for national subsidies in both England and France, we would have to shoot the entire film in both languages.

This we could not afford. I went back to Hallam Street with a bottle of champagne. "What are we celebrating" I was asked?

I replied "it's a wrap party."

I sold the script to Michael Winner, who promptly and smartly, sold it to an investor. The picture was never made. What a pity.

I've devoted this book to my career and the many films I have made. The ones I remember best are, frankly, those that I didn't make, for one reason or another. Some of them I may make still.

For instance I am hopeful that we will make *Moll Flanders* with Ken Russell as the director.

After many delays, which have extended over a period of some thirty years, I had hoped to make *Moll Flanders* this past year. I had managed to persuade, Barry Humphries, to play the famous Madame who appears in the film. Barry is the delightful Australian comic, who is best known for playing Dame Edna.

I had a most entertaining dinner with Ken Russell and Lisi his wife as well as Barry and his wife. We had so many laughs. But we haven't made the picture yet, due to a shortfall in the available finances

Last year, I also planned to make a picture about Mary Read. It is the true story of a pirate, who really lived in the Caribbean, some three hundred years ago. I happened to see a play once, staged in London with, Robert Donat and Flora Robson. Alexander Korda was involved and he, obviously, intended this play to, ultimately, become a film. The film was never made.

After writing a new script, I was quite close to getting the picture off the ground. I had arranged for the shooting of the pirate sequences to be done in the same tank facilities, in the Bahamas, which had been used for the two sequels to *Pirates of the Caribbean*.

Unfortunately, due to pre-production delays, we would have run into the typhoon season, which made our Completion Guarantors nervous about the potential risk. Although I was very unhappy, we'll try again, next year.

I also had the rights, through the Noël Coward Estate, to Noël's play *Present Laughter*, which has never been filmed and could have been shot anywhere. The problem here was finding a suitable cast, with the necessary star value.

I discussed with the Coward estate the book written by Sheridan Morley, under the title *A Talent To Amuse*. The book is, basically, a biography of Noël Coward.

I had a thought of using Sheridan Morley as the host and making the film, what I would call, a docudrama, dealing not only with Coward and his music, his songs sung by himself, as well as, scenes from some of the films with which he was associated.

Sheridan Morley is alas no longer with us.

Then, I have *Tammany Hall*, which I am hoping to make next year, probably in Connecticut. This is the story of Boss Tweed, the corrupt, but also much loved politician, who was, in part, responsible for such New York landmarks as the Brooklyn Bridge.

I also wrote a script last year, on a subject that's always been close to my heart. I am fascinated with the life and works of Oscar Wilde.

I am aware that a very good film, *Wilde*, was made some years ago, but there are aspects of Oscar Wilde's life which are not fully covered. I intended to base the script I wrote on the last years of Oscar Wilde's life, starting with the beginning of his trial, which ended so tragically, and finally his death.

I have a great title for the film, which comes from, what I consider one of the best paragraphs in English literature. The paragraph comes from *De Profundis*, which was written in the form of a letter, from Reading Jail.

The line which I am quoting from memory is:

"All trials are trials for ones life, just as all sentences are sentences of death. I have been tried three times and on the last occasion, was sent to prison for two years of hard labor.

"Society, as we have constituted it, will have no place for me, has none to offer; but Nature, whose sweet rains fall on unjust and just alike, will have clefts in the rocks where I may hide, and secret valleys in whose silence I may weep undisturbed. She will hang the night with stars so that I may walk abroad in the darkness without stumbling, and send the wind over my footprints so that none may track me to my hurt ...."

I just want to call the movie *Hang the Night with Stars*.

Talking of good ideas; I had another thought while in St. Petersburg with Michael Caine. How about remaking the film based on the play *The Entertainer*?

The play was all about a vaudeville comic. It was clear, from Laurence Oliver's version, that Archie Rice, the name of the principle character, was based on a rather objectionable comic, such as Max Miller. My suggestion to Michael was that he should make it a softer and more pleasant role, more in the style of *Alfie* and base his performance on Tommy Trinder, (whom I mentioned earlier in this book).

Michael Caine thought about it very carefully and then said, "Harry. I'm afraid the answer is no. I don't want to be compared to Laurence Olivier." Well that was his decision and another good idea went west.

On another subject; I knew the late Harry Lauder, because in the hay days of my radio empire I had the idea of doing a radio show with Harry. He was a good friend and was always doing final tours. My idea was to do the final tour on radio.

So we went to see Sir Harry Lauder. He had a wonderful house, somewhere between Glasgow and Edinburgh. When you first entered the house, there was an enormous stairway and, at the top of it, hung a portrait of Sir Harry's son, Capt. John Lauder, in the full dress uniform of an officer in a Scottish Highland Regiment. Sir Harry's son John had been killed during World War One

This had a great effect on Sir Harry and on the rest of his life. He wrote the song "Keep Right on 'til the End of the Road", which after the classics such "Tipperary" and "Pack Up Your Troubles" was the marching song of the British Army in France, during the closing stages of World War One. It so much typified Harry Lauder, that I always remembered it. I didn't manage to persuade Sir Harry to do the radio series, but quite recently, I had the thought of dramatizing Sir Harry's life story. He was the first vaudeville artist from the UK, to have a world wide success. Sir Harry was handled by the famous, William Morris, of the Morris Agency, so there were a lot of famous people involved in his life.

I had the idea of using Billy Connelly to play Harry Lauder. Unfortunately, when I contacted the Harry Lauder estate they thought it was a very nice idea, but were totally against Billy Connelly. Once again I had had a good idea that wasn't going to work

Now reverting to the present day. I have been using an escort agency in the London area with the delightful name of "A Touch of Class."

To give you some idea how prices have changed in all walks of life. The going rate for a first class "escort" is two hundred and fifty pounds per hour, or one thousand pounds per night. (In the1950 the 'price of vice' was about one third of this amount.)

If you look at the current value of the pound compared to the US dollar you will see that the price of vice has become considerably more expensive in London than it is, currently, in New York.

The constant addition of Eastern European States to the European Union has provided for this agency, as well as its competitors, a constant supply of new talent, who come to London to make money.

Another little story about, "A Touch of Class."

A couple of years ago, I had the pleasure of meeting a young, most charming lady from the agency, who came from Indonesia and used the name Bali. Bali came with me to Cannes, where she was a great success and everyone was enormously impressed with her beauty, talent and intelligence. As Bali had to return to London before me, I asked her if I should arrange for a car to meet her.

"No, thank you," she said. "I have already arranged for a car to meet me; won't cost me anything either, 'cause the driver owes me a favor."

"What do you mean, owes you a favor," I asked.

"I had a client, a Saudi Arabian Prince, who wanted the pleasure of seeing me attacked in the posterior by a black gentleman. So, my friend, the driver preformed as asked, for the fee of one thousand pounds. I think he owes me a favor, don't you?"

Well one person's favor can be another person's destruction.

Take garbage for example. Contrary to some opinion, "garbage" can play a role in movie making

For instance, in the original version of Noel Coward's wartime masterpiece, *In Which We Serve,* there is a scene early on in the film when the destroyer that played such a vital role in the story was launched; an important item was featured among the "garbage."

It was the front page of the Daily Express bearing the headline, "There Will Be No War."

Lord Beaverbrook, who owned the Express group of newspapers was so furious that he ordained that Noel Coward's name should never even appear in any of his newspapers. In a print of the film that I recently saw on television, the "garbage" had been removed.

Another much happier use of "garbage" in a film was in *Casablanca.*

In the scene toward the end of the film where the German General, played by Conrad Veidt, gets shot by Humphrey Bogart, we see among the "garbage" a prominently labelled empty bottle of Vichy Water, a clear reference to the French government of the time, who were collaborating with the Germans.

Chapter Fifteen
All the Spoons
in All the Glasses

I am suffering from frustration.
   I have no cure in sight.
   Everybody I call is on voicemail.
Nobody calls me back.
I have emails to send, all composed in my mind, but I don't want to send them until I have some news.
I think it will be good news, but fear it will be bad.
Even if it is good news, this won't be the end of the affair.
Just the beginning of another ten days or more of frantic work to maybe achieve a "closing."
Last night I had a nightmare.
The nightmare is over now and I am back to reality.
Reality is far worse than the nightmare.
I just wish I could fall asleep.
Shakespeare, as usual, said it all:
"To be or not to be—that is the question?"
He did not have the answer.
And neither have I, so I'll make another phone call.
All humanity can't be on voicemail.
Not all—just the ones to whom I need to talk.
Frustration—that's part of life

Although, I have made movies all around the world and have had a home in New York for some years, my movie making in the United States has been very limited and confined to Los Angeles and New York.
I have spent time in Atlanta, Boston, Chicago, Cincinnati, Las Vegas, Miami,

New Orleans and San Francisco and I am also very familiar with the Caribbean Islands. Until a few months ago, I had never visited Detroit, Michigan.

Detroit is connected directly to Canada with a bridge and a tunnel.

My present home in Toronto is less than thirty minutes by cab from the airport.

The flight is fifty minutes and then it's about half an hour to the City Center of Detroit where I love to stay at the Detroit Marriott Renaissance hotel—all in all a total of less than two hours.

Allowing for the currently devalued U.S. dollar, America is one of the cheapest and certainly the best country in the world to make movies.

Of all the states, Michigan offers the highest incentive of 42% as well as a valuable loan program. That is what brought me here, for the first time in my life a couple of months ago.

I have found the citizens of Detroit to be very kind and welcoming to strangers (such as myself) as well as very talented—wonderful people. Their ambitions are simple—to make Michigan a rival Hollywood in its contribution to movie making in the U.S.A. and the rest of the world. I am doing my best to help.

I am about to start shooting on *Pickton*, the true story of a serial killer who, in Vancouver, BC. Canada, murdered twenty-seven young girls whose bodies he fed to the pigs on the farm where he lived. He was arrested in 2002 but because the evidence was based purely on DNA, he was only tried and sentenced to life in prison at the end of 2007.

Hence it is only now that this horrific tale can be told.

Pickton will be portrayed by an old friend of mine, Robert Englund. He has worked with me in three previous films produced in Budapest (Hungary), Tel Aviv (Israel) and Johannesburg (South Africa). Robert who lives in Los Angeles will probably feel more at home in Detroit.

After Pickton is completed I hope to produce and appear in a series of twelve documentaries entitles "How to Make a Movie." The shows will consist of exerts from the one hundred plus movies I have made as well as twelve Michigan Film Students whose questions about film making I shall do my best to answer.

In November, with the help of the Michigan government, I hope to establish and fully equip the first facility in Detroit, able to fully produce electronic video games, currently one of the most profitable arms of the movie industry. I am already working on my very first video game.

I am rather proud of my ability in finding original titles for films.

I'll type out on my computer the Title Page, complete with all the essential copyright information.

I know that the Final Page traditionally ends with

FADE TO BACK

ROLL CLOSING TITLES

It's the pages in between that are the problem,

Sometimes, I'll write a treatment, running from a minimum of two to as many as twenty pages.

Then, I shall bring in a co-writer to complete the first draft screenplay.

My excuse is that I find it difficult to objectively criticize my own work. In my early days I usually wrote everything myself. I couldn't afford to pay a co-writer.

I've produced a lot of movies. Sometimes it seems that I only became a film producer to sell the rights in the screenplays which I wrote, or co-wrote.

And that's the truth, pure and simple.

As Oscar Wilde, my favorite co-writer, once said. "The truth is rarely pure and never simple. Modern life would be very tedious if it were either, and modern literature a complete impossibility"

Epilogue
Au Revoir – Not Goodbye

As I look back on a long and active life, I realize that I have ridden a roller coaster between triumph and disaster. The Gods have been kind to me. I can only pray they continue to do so. In the words of Mr. Micawber, I can only keep going, in the optimistic belief that "something will turn up."

Meantime, in addressing Maria, I can only echo the words of the great Cockney comedian, Albert Chevalier: "We've been together now for forty years, an' it don't seem a day to much, there ain't a lady livin' in the land, as I'd swap for my dear old Dutch."

I haven't mentioned my father since the first chapter. He was a well known theatrical manager and I have noticed quite recently, that a third London theatre has been named after a famous, contemporary actor. The three theatres are Laurence Olivier, John Gielgud and now Noël Coward.

All three of them were under contract to me at some time. I would like to think, that whatever I may have achieved, my father would be proud of me for this.

Earlier on, under the subject of the London Night Spot, the Cabaret Club, I have mentioned the Profumo Affair. This famous affair took place in London, within one year of my own disastrous involvement with Miss Novotny in New York. For those who remember the details of the Profumo affair, or saw the movie *Scandal*, the name of Dr. Stephen Ward will be familiar.

I never met Stephen Ward, but he was once pointed out to me at a reception in London. I noticed then, that he was accompanied by several attractive young ladies. As you may recall, he committed suicide during the closing stages of his trial, in fear of a guilty verdict and prison sentence.

Our basic cases were very similar, as both were based on the accusation of profiting from the earning of a call girl. Dr. Ward chose to die by his own hand. I sought another route, based on the old proverb—"He who fights and runs away, lives to fight another day."

However, every time I go from Central London to the airport, I pass Marylebone Magistrate's Court, where Dr. Ward's ordeal began.

I mentally raise my hat to his memory. He died—I lived—and am still fighting.

I still hope to make some of the movies I have talked about. Perhaps I will, perhaps I won't, but whatever I do I shall keep on working, because I know no other life. At the beginning of this book, I mentioned that I first started to make money by writing gags, for comics, in vaudeville acts.

The many times I saw the late and great Jimmy (Schnozzle) Durante perform I could not help but identify with the line: "I should have stayed in Vaudeville."

The English language is a treasure trove of opportunities and inspiration for the professional gag writer. For instance, at all times, you should be very careful when eating breakfast. After all you never know when a plate of cornflakes may turn into a "cereal (serial) killer."

Another example, in my early days as a provider of material for the American Vaudeville Act of 'Forsythe, Seamon and Farrell', little Addi Seamon proudly displayed the latest gift from her boyfriend—a diamond wristwatch. When her teammate Elanor Farrell, after having examined the watch, proclaimed that the watch had nothing on the inside, Addi promptly responded, "Don't worry, my boyfriend said that tomorrow night he would give me the "works."

It is only appropriate to end with a vaudeville story

There used to be a wonderful vaudeville conjurer, Gaston Palmer. Gaston used to go through his act, which was not bad, just mediocre and every so often his beautiful assistant would hand him a prop to perform with.

It consisted of a tray, on which there where ten glasses and ten spoons.

Gaston would toss the tray in the air and catch it as if fell and there would always be three or four, on some occasion there would be as many as 6 spoons in the glasses.

Finishing his act to pleasant applause, Gaston, would, as if by inspiration, (remember he had been doing this act in theaters or night clubs for at least 25 years), toss the tray into the air once more and, when it came down again Gaston had finally done it—Ten spoons resting in ten glasses.

Gaston would hold the tray up in the air and march triumphantly around the night club, or, if it was a theater, the stalls.

While the orchestra played "The March Loraine" Gaston used to cry out in triumph, "ALL THE SPOONS IN ALL THE GLASSES!"

That is the way I would like to go out: "ALL THE SPOONS IN ALL THE GLASSES."

I have, as yet, not managed to get all the spoons in all the glasses, but as long as I am alive I will keep on trying.

Post Script

Winston Churchill once observed that democracy is not the easiest way of fighting a war, but in the end, it's the best available.

Britain and the United States, in their respective histories, have shared the same experiences. Britain suffered a Civil War, the Cavaliers versus the Roundheads, followed by the trial and execution of its King, Charles the First

After a comparatively brief reign by the Lord Protector, Oliver Cromwell, Britain welcomed the Restoration of Charles the Second with a mixture of joy and relief. The United States has, so far, only experienced a Civil War, in which the right cause triumphed.

Americans should be very grateful.

Let's hope that the future holds no prospect of further sad experiences.

God Bless America and our wonderful little space ship Planet Earth

All countries have their faults, but again, considering all the alternatives, it's the best game in town.

Now, let's look forward to the distant future.

Writers of science fiction from Jules Verne to H.G. Wells have endeavored to give us their vision. As is so often the case, a study of the past contains for the future two alternatives—pessimism and optimism.

In ancient times mankind sought spiritual help from a multitude of deities. It would appear that the Hebrews were the first to accept only one God as their spiritual leader. Christ was born a Jew, and, in the Christian religion, the Old Testament is based solely on the Hebrew version of history.

Just a few hundred years after the death of Christ, Mohammed was born and, in turn, taught his followers to accept the singularity of one God, known as Allah. Thus, it is the conflict between Hebrews, Christians and Muslims that is at the root cause of the problems, not only of the Middle East, but also in the rest of the world.

Some, who claim to have vision, believe that the economic future of the world may be in the hands of China, and, to a lesser extent, India.

If we take an optimistic view of the future, we must all pray that one day, alas, all too probably hundreds of years from now, a Jew, a Christian and a Muslim may kneel down together, possibly in outer space, and worship in unity, one God. After all it is one and the same energy that created all of life.

Then, the trio will make peace with their economic partners in Asia and it may be truly said that the Pax Universal is accepted by the entire world.

We can only hope the Pax Americana can survive way beyond our own lifetimes, to be, ultimately, we hope and pray, replaced by the Pax Universal.

That's the optimistic view of "THE SHAPE OF THINGS TO COME."

What's the pessimistic view?

Possibly a nuclear Third World War, in which each side completely exterminates the other.

Want to bet on it?

The stakes are high—the future of all life on Earth, which includes the human race.

To quote William Saroyan: "it's a great day for the race."

"What race?" was the question.

The reply, in universal unity, is loud and clear:

"THE HUMAN RACE."

To Maria

The book is ended but our life together goes on.
Side by side we have lived together a life of excitement and discovery.
We both know now and are in complete agreement that we love each other
with constancy and passion.
Whatever the future may have in store, this enduring love will continue to sustain us.
I hope and wish that one day we will Rest in Peace together side by side in London
Our love will outlive us both.
It is the love of eternity.

§

Index

A

Adams, Paul 55
Adorf, Mario 56, *73*
Adventures of the Scarlet Pimpernel, The 29, 40
African Queen, The 126
Agrama, Frank 115-116
Alfie 129
Alexander the Great 124
Ambler, Eric 124
Ameche, Don 110-111
Amies, Hardy 8
Anatomist, The 40
Andrews, Julie 8, 47
Andrews Sisters, The 15
Andrews, Ted 8
Anglade, France 55
Annakin, Ken *77*, 91
Annals of the British institute for Psychic Research, The 40
Anthony and Cleopatra 38
Arkoff, Sam 57, 59
Armbrister, Lolita 104-105, 106
Arnaz, Desi 38
Around the World in 80 Days 21, 37
Askey, Arthur 9

Astaire, Fred 9
A Talent To Amuse 128
Attenborough, Richard 18, 96
Audran, Stéphane 96
Frankie Avalon 56
Aviator. The 36
Aza, Bert 122
Aznavour, Charles 15, 96, 97

B

Babe 123
Bacall, Lauren 21
Bali 130
Ball, Lucille 38
Banks, Monty 35
Barker, Eric 20
Barker, Lex 53, 54
Barker, Vedrenne 1
Beaverbrook, Lord 130
Beecham, Sir Thomas 20
Belle, Annie 97-100
Bennett, Mr. 2
Benson, Juliette 120
Berger, Senta 56
Bergin, Patrick 116, 124
Bergman, Ingrid 57, 91
Bernard Brothers The 15
Billy, Madame 16
Black, George, 7
Black Arrow. 105
Black Museum, The 29
Black Velvet – White Silk 98-99
Blair, Tony X
Bogart, Humphrey 21, 130
Bond, Timothy 116
Borgnine, Ernest 106
Booth, Webster 19
Boyfriend, The 47
Braden, Bernard 29
Bragg, Melvyn 102
Brauner, Arthur 88, 89
Brides of Fu Manchu, The 56, **74**
Bridge on the River Kwai, The 126
Brook, Clive 14
Brown, Gordon, X

Bulganin, Nikolai 26, 27
Bullet to Beijing 49, 50, **86**, 119
Bush, George W. X
Byron, Lord 19

C
Cabaret 28
Caine, Michael 119, 121, 129
Calamity Club, The 8-9
Caldwell, Henry 40
Caligula 101, 121
Call of the Wild, The **77,** 91, 95-96
Campbell Jones, Paddy 14
Cantinflas 37
Carey, Joyce 18
Casablanca 130
Castle of Fu Manchu, The 89
Castro, Fidel 123
Ceasar and Cleopatra 38
Celi, Adolfo 96
Chaliapin, Feodor 20
Chamberlain, Joseph IX
Chamberlain, Neville X
Charteris, Leslie 48, 124
Chevalier, Maurice 15
Chin, Tsai 56
Chow, Raymond 57, 58
Christian, Linda 89
Christie, Agatha 55, 96, 113, 124
Churchill, Winston X, 7, 8, 19, 31, 117, 137
Churchill, Mrs. Winston 6
Circus of Fear 56
Citizen Kane 22
City of Fear 53-54, 123
Clark, Fred 58
Clark, Petula 19, 127
Clark, Robert 53
Claude, Madame 16, 57-58
Clinton, Hilary 117
Coast of Skeletons 54, 106-107
Cochran, Steve 54
Cockleshell Heroes 31
~~Cohen, Harry 21-22~~
Cohen, Nat 90, 91, 92
Cohn, Harry 21, 22

Colicos, John 100
Collins, Norman 40, 43
Comfort, John 46
Command Performance 37
Connelly, Billy 129
Cornfeld, Bernie 59
Costa, Sam 9
Cott, Ted 30
Cotton, Joseph 60
Coward, Noel ~~3, 7,~~ 2, 6, 13-14, 18-19, 22, 96, 110, 128, 130, 135
Craig, Mae 21
Crawford, Broderick 40, 47
Crime Club 47-48
Cromwell, James 123
Crosby, Bing ~~10,~~ 9, 13, 33
Cross, Chris 40
Cry the Beloved Country 117
Cummings, Robert 56, *75*
Curtis, Tony 116

D

Dallamano, Massimo 89, 97
Dan Dare – Pilot of the Future 20
Daniels, Gary 124, 126
Danning, Sybil 106
Darren, James *76*, 97
Darwin, Charles 126
Da Vinci, Elena 46
Davis, Colonel, 54
Dean, Basil 3
Death Deceit & Destiny Aboard the Orient Express 124
Deigton, Len 117
DeMille, Cecil B. 13, 99
Depp, Johnny 40
De Sade, Marquis 89
Desert Victory 45
Desmond, Florence 32
DIAL 999 46-47
Diamond Cut Diamond. 126
Dickens, Charles 34, 48, 117
Dickinson, Angie *79, 80*, 101
Dietz, Howard 37
Disney, Walt 13, 105
Don Quixhote. 2, 45
D'Oyly Carte, Rupert 1

Donat, Robert 30, 128
Donlevy, Brian 56
Dorian 124
Doyle, Sir Arthur Conan 29, 114, 126
Dragnet 44
Dragonard 107-108
Duchess of Kent, 18
Duda, Matthew, 119
Dudikoff, Michael 108, 109, 113
Duke of Windsor 26
Dunaway, Faye 121
Duncan, Ian 124
Duvivier, Julien 126

E

Eagle, S.P. 126
East, Jeff *81*, 101
Eastman, George 95
Eastwood, Clint 95
Eaton, Shirley 56, *73*
Eden, Sir Anthony 9
Ekland, Brit 90, 100
Elliot, Madge 8
Empty House, The 29
Englund, Robert 114, 117, 132
Entertainer, The 129
Eugenie 90, 92
Eve 58-59, 104

F

Fabian 56
Fabian of the Yard 19
Face of Fu Manchu, The 56, *71*
Fanny Hill 84, 101-105, 117
Feldman, Ed 56
Ferratti, Rebecca 106
Ferrer, Tony 58
Field, Sid 7
Fields, Gracie 7, 8, 14, 19, 29, 33, 34, 35, 122
Finch, Peter 14
Fire Over England 10
Fistful of Dollars 89, 95
Fitzgerald, Barry 21
Five Golden Dragons 56, *75*, 88

Fleming, Ian 124
Flynn, Errol 38
Fontaine. Lynn 1, 6
Forrester, C.S. 21, 29
Foster, Jodie 102
Four Musketeers, The 88
Franco, Jess 45, 59, 89, 90
Franks, Jack 15
Fraser, Sir Robert 40. 43
Freed, Alan 47
Fröbe, Gert 56, 96
From Hell 40
Fu Manchu 55
Furst, Austin 106, 121
Fyffe, Will 122

G

Gail, Zoe 7
Gamel, Nadia 55
Gammell, Robin, 101
Garfield Weston, Willard 25
Gargan, William 46
Garson, Greer 37, 40
Gaudi, Antoni 89
Gazarra, Ben 47
Genn, Leo 56, *73*
George, Doro 25
Gere, Richard 113
Gibbons, Rodney 123.
Gielgud, Sir John 29-30, 135
Gingold, Hermione 7, 40
Girl From Rio, The 59
Giuliani, Mayor Rudy 16
Globus, Yoram 105, 108, 116
Godoy, Valentina 59
Golan, Menaham 105, 106, 108
Golden, Herb 21
Golden Years of Sherlock Holmes, The 29-30, 115, 116
Goldman, Harold 59
Gomez, Andres Vicente 16, 91-93
Goodbye Mr. Chips 30
Good Companions, The 19
Gor 106
Goring, Marius 29, 40
Gracie Fields Show, The 14

Grade, Leslie 26, 43
Grade, Lew 26, 43, 44, 47
Grade, Michael 26
Graham, Billy 44
Grant. Cary 126
Green, Nigel 55
Greene, Graham 22, 124
Greene, Lorne 23, *79, 82, 101*
Grenfell, Joyce 13
Grieco, Richard 124
Griffith. Thomas Ian 124
Guccione, Bob 101, 120, 121

H

Hackney. Pearl 20
Haggard, Rider 100, 124
Hang the Night with Stars 129
Happy and Glorious 7
Hardwick, Edward 124
Harris, Richard, 117
Harrison, Rex 18, 90
Harwood, Ronald 117
Haskin, Byron 32
Hayworth, Rita 21, 22
Heasman, Ernie 34
Henry V 38
Heston, Charlton 60, 91
High Adventure 51, 124
High Explosive 124
Higham, David 22, 49
Hildegarde 33
Hipwell, Reggie 15-16
Hitchcock, Alfred 30, 125
Holloway, Stanley 21, 47, 56, *73*, 122, 127
Holt, Renate 57
Hooper, Tobe 116, 117
Hope, Bob 33
Hopkins, Anthony 102
Horatio Hornblower 21, 29
Horne, Kenneth 9
Horwitz, Lew 114, 117, 123
Hot Cinders 3
Hough, John 91, 105
House of a Thousand Dolls 58
Howard, Leslie 7, 8, 10

Howard, Trevor 31-32
Howsam, Gary 124
Hughes, Howard 36, 54
Humphries, Barry 128
Hyde-White, Wilfred 56, *73*, 100, 102
Hyer. Martha 58
Hylton, Jack 36, 37

I

I Am A Camera 28
I Love Lucy 38, 44
Incident at Victoria Falls, The 116
ITMA – It's That Man Again 4

J

Jackson, Douglas 120
Jackson, Glenda, 102
Jeffries, Lionel 56, 127
Jones, James Earl 117
Jones, Josephine Jacqueline (J.J.) 104-105, 106
Jones, R.G. 2, 47
Justined 89

K

Karas, Anton 22
Kavanagh, Ted 4
Keaton, Buster 127
Keeler, Christine 25
Kamp, Alexandra 126
Kennedy, John F. 46, 88
Kerr Deborah 37
Khashoggi, Adnan 104-105
Khrushchev 26-27
King Edward III, IX
King Edward VII 116
King Farouk of Egypt 55
King George V, X
King George VI,X
King Kong 125, 126
King of Bulgaria 124
King of Diamonds, 47
King Solomon's Mines 100, 106
King Solomon's Treasure 100, 106-107

King, Stephen 116-117
Kinski, Klaus 56, 89, 90
Kipling, Rudyard 125
Kitt, Eartha 107
Klondike Fever **79, 80, 81, 82, 83,** 101-102, 124
Korda, Sir Alexander ~~10,~~ 9, 22-23, 29, 53, 117, 128
Khrushchev, Nikita 26, 27
Kunz, Charlie 19

L

Lady from Shanghai, The 21-22
Lamour, Dorothy 33
Lamping, Frank 5, 17
Langtry, Lilly 116
Lauder, Harry 129
Laughton, Charles 10
Laurence of Arabia 126
Lavi, Dahlia 56, *73*
Lawrence, Gertrude 2
Lawrence of Arabia 117
Lax, Leo 87
Lean, David 126
Lee, Christopher 55, 56, 58, *71*, 90, 115
Lee, Margaret 56
Leigh, Vivien 38
Lenfilms 120
Lerner, Avi 106
Lewinsky, Monica 37
Liberace 44
~~*Life of Harry Lime, The* 22-23, 29~~
Lilli Palmer Playhouse ~~40,~~ 90
Lilli Palmer Presents. 40
Lilly, Beatrice 28
Lisbon Story 7
Little. Billy 32
Littler, Prince 40
Lives of Harry Lime, The 22-23, 29
Lloyd, Harold 36
Lloyd, Marie 35, 36
Lom, Herbert 56, 59, 89, 90, 106, 109
London, Jack 91, 101-102, 124
London Playhouse 14, 19, 21
London Story, The 19
Lost World, The 116, 126
Louis, Victor 49

Lucan, Arthur 4, 7
Lunt, Alfred 6
Lynn, Robert 46
Lynn, Dame Vera 9, 19

M

MacCambridge, Mercedes 59
MacDonald, David 45
Maclean, Stuart 45
MacMillan, Harold 25
Macnee, Patrick 100, 115
Macpherson, Stewart 20
Maisky, Ivan Mikhailovich 20
Mandela, Nelson 117
Mangler, The 117
Mankowitz, Wolf 45
Manley, Walter 110
Mantovani 13
Mantovani, 47
March, Fredric, 47
March of the Movies 6, 8, 10, 11, 13
Marco Polo 123
Markle, Fletcher 21
Marlow, Pat 36-37
Marshall, Zena 55
Martin Kane, 46
Marx, Groucho 127
Maschwitz, Eric 6
Mason, James 21, 122
Master of Dragonard Hill, 107
May, Karl 53
McCallum, David 100
McCormack, Eric 116
McDowell, Malcolm 124
McShane, Kitty 4, 7
Mediterranean Merry-Go-Round 20
Meredith, Burgess 110-111
Merman, Ethel 36
Merrick, David 28
Meyer, Richard 17, 44
Midnight in St. Petersburg 119
Mihalka, George 120
Miller, Margaret (mother) VII, 1-2, 3, 4-5, 6, 9, 11, 19, 25, 26, 27, 33, 36, 37, 39-41,
	45, 46, 48, 49, *61, 62,* 88
Miller, Max 34, 129

Mills, John 19
Mitchell, Leslie 8, 11, 13
Moby Dick 45
Moll Flanders 121, 128
Monroe, Marilyn 37, 38
Montand, Yves 15
Montés, Eliza 59
Moore, Terry 53
Morgan, Andre 57
Morley, Robert 102
Morley, Sheridan 128
Morse, Barry 101
Mosley, Oswald 2
Mountbatten, Lord Louis X
Mouse Trap, The 55
Much Binding in the Marsh 9, 20, 120
Mummy, The 116
Murdoch, Sir Keith 14, 45
Murdoch, Richard 9
Murdoch, Rupert 14
Murray, Percival 25-26, 46
Murrow, Ed 5
My Fair Lady 21, 47
My Family and Other Animals 57, 91

N

Nader, George 58
Navy Lark. The 20
Neagle, Anna 14, 31, 32
Necronomicon 59
Neeson, Liam 10
Neff, Hildegard 54
Nicholson, Jack 121
Nidorf, Mike 43
Night of the High Tide 99-100
99 Women 59-60, 110
Noël Coward Show, The 13
Norris, Aaron 109
Northcliffe. Lord 125
Novotny, Mariella 48, 90, 110, 135

O

Oakroyd, Jess *19*
O'Brian, Hugh 56, **73**

O'Hara, Gerry 102, 116
Oh Mistress Mine 7
Oliver Twist 34
Olivier, Laurence 10, 30, 38, 45, 129, 135
On the Waterfront 126
Origin of the Species. 126
Othello 22, 29
Our Man in Marrakesh 56
Outlaw of Gor, 106
Owd Bob 122, 123
Owen, Tristram 23, 90

P

Pacey, Tom 122
Packer, Frank 45
Packwood, Charles 1, 2
Palance, Jack *78*, 89, 96, 98, 101, 106, 123
Palmer, Lillie 40, 90
Parker, Colonel 123
Payn, Graham 13
Pearce, Christopher 108, 109, 114
Peck, Gregory 21, 45
Peers, Donald 19, 36
Performer, The 122
Perkins, Anthony 113, 116
Peron, Evita 17
Perretti, Giancarlo 113-114
Personal Call, 6
Peter Pan 32
Phoenix, Hunter VII
Piaf, Edith 15
Pickles, Wilfred 19
Pickton 132
Picture of Dorian Gray, The 89-90
Pilgrim's Progress, 10
Pinsent, Gordon *83*, 101
Pirate's Curse. The 124
Pirates of the Caribbean 128
Pitt, Archie 122
Platoon Leader 108, 109
Pleasance, Donald 105, 106
Plowright, Joan 45
Polanski, Roman 121
Post, Ted 47
Power, Romina 89

Power, Tyrone 89
Present Laughter, 128
Presley, Elvis 123
Price, Dennis 56, **73**
Price, Vincent 58
Prince Charles, X
Prince William, X
Princess Diana, X
Priestley, J.B. 19-20, 124
Private Live of Henry VIII, The 10

Q
Queen Elizabeth II, X, 27, 120
Queen Mary, X
Queen's Messenger 124, 126
Queen Salote of Tonga, 19
Queen Victoria, IX, 32, 35

R
Raft, George 56, 114
Raley, Ron 113
Rampling, Charlotte 102
Randall, Tony 56
Rank, J. Arthur 9, 10
Rathbone, Basil 40
Rattigan, Terence 7-20 6, 19
Redgrave, Michael 21, 29
Reed, Oliver 96, 102, 105, 106-107, 123
Rey, Fernando 105
Rhys-Davies, John 116
Rice Davies, Mandy 25
Richardson, Ralph 20, 29-30
Ritchard, Cyril 8
River of Death 108, 109
Robson, Flora 128
Rocket to the Moon 7, 56-57
Roeg, Nicholas 51, 91
Rogers, Captain Kelly 31
Rohmer, Sax 55, 56
Rohm, Maria VII, 34, 49, 54, 56, 57, 58, 59, 60, **69**, **75**, **76**, 87, 88, 89, 90, 93, 96, 97, 98, 101, 103, 104, 110, 135
Rohmer, Sax 55, 56
Ronald, Tom 3
Roodt, Darrell 126

Rooney, Mickey 54-55, 108, 123
Roosevelt, Franklin D. X, 8
Roosevelt, Theodore 116
Roper, Mark 123
Rosenkrantz, Ed 16-17
Ross, Edmondo 19
Rothermere, Lord 14, 18, 33
Rowe, Peter 123
Russell, Ken 102, 121, 128
Russell, Lisi 128

S

~~Sbariga, Giulio 95-96, 102~~
Safety Last 36
Salkind, Alexander 87-88
Saltzman, Harry 119
Sanders, George 59, 89
Sanders of the River 53
Sandy the Seal 4
Sbariga, Giulio 95-96, 102
Sea Wolf, The 124
Scandal 90, 135
Scarlet Pimpernel, The 10, 29
Schell, Maria 59
Scott, Macgregor 87
Scott, Ridley, 44
Scrimgeour, C.G. 14
Secrets of Scotland Yard, 14, 29
Sellers, Peter 60
Selznick, David O. 22-23, ~~29~~ 28
Shakespeare, William 2, 29, 38, 131
Shakira, 120
Shape of Things to Come, The **78**, 101
Sharp, Don 57
Shaw, George Bernard 1, 38,
Shaw, Sir Run Run 57, 58
She 124
Sherlock Holmes 29
Shulman, Milton 29
Signoret, Simone 15
Sim, Alistair 40
Simmons, Jean 33, 37
Simons, Ed 117
Singh, Anant 117
Skeleton Coast, 106

Slezak, Walter 54, 90, 91, 92
Sommer, Elke 96
Sosenko, Anna 33
Southwood, Lord 34
Spiegel, Sam 126
Spreading the News 21
Stander, Lionel 91, 92
Standing, John 124, 126
Stanelli, 8
Stanley, C.O. 40
Stark, Ray 21
Steiger, Rod *79*, *81*, 101
Stevenson, Robert Louis 91, 105, 113, 123
Stodel, John 106
Sturges, Preston 36
Sullivan, Ed 40, 41
Sultan of Zanzibar 19
Sumuru 56, 59, 126
Sunday Night at the Palladium 44
Sundowner. The 14
Superman 87-88, 101
Sweet and Low 7

T

Table Bay 53
Tales from Dickens, 47
Tales From Manhattan 126
Tamiroff, Akim 45, 89
Tammany Hall 128
Tasca, Prince Alesandro 115
Taxi, 50
Ten Little Indians 55-56, *73*, 96, 113, 115
Terry-Thomas 56, 100, 127
Thatcher, Margaret X
There is no Business like Show Business 36
They Never Let Me Finish It 45
Third Man, The 21-22
Thirty Nine Steps, The 30
Thomas, Howard 9, ~~51~~ 50
Thornton Smith, Ernest 25
Three Musketeers, The 88
Todd, Mike 21, 37
Todd, Richard 53, 54, 90, 116
Torch, Sidney 5
Touch of Evil, A 113, 116

Towers, Harry P. (father) VII, 1, 2, 3, 20, 25, 31, 100, 107, 135
Treasure Island 91-92, 123
Tree, Sir Herbert Beerbohm 1, 81, 107, 147 (same line)
Trinder, Tommy 7, 15, 27, 36, 100, 129
Troob, Warren 47
Tweed, Boss 128
Twenty Four Hours to Kill 54-55

U

Unger, Oliver 54, 55, 59, 60, 88
Ustinov, Peter 60

V

Vaughan, Robert 106-107, 109
Veidt, Conrad 130
Vengeance of Fu Manchu, The 56, 58
Venus in Furs **76**, 97
Verne, Jules 22, 56, 137

W

Walker Jr., Robert 58
Wall, Max 5
Wallace, Edgar 53, 56, 125-126
Walters, Barbara 39
Walters, Lou 39
Ward, Dr. Stephen 135-136
Warner, David, 116
Warner, Jack 37
Wasserman, Lew 44
Welles, Orson 21-22, 29-30, 45, 91-92, 107
Wells, H.G. 92, 101, 137
Werba, Hank 105
White, Frank, 46\
Wilby, Fred 18
Wilcox, Herbert 10, 31-32
Wilde 128
Wilde, Oscar 89, 124, 128-129, 133
Wilder. Billy 110
Willis, Bruce 113
Winner, Michael 127, 128
Winston, Harry 31
Winter, Ophelia 124
Winters, Shelley **84**, 102

Wolfit, Sir Donald 117
World's Greatest Mysteries, The 40

Y

Yankalevich, Jaime 17
Yarnell, Celeste 58-59, 104
You'll Never See Me Again 47
You Never Can Tell 1

Z

Zanger, Ziggy 98-99
Ziegler, Anne 19

CPSIA information can be obtained at www.ICGtesting.com
Printed in the USA
LVOW100308130213

319727LV00008B/355/P